SOUTACHE

First published in Great Britain 2017 by Search Press Limited,
Wellwood, North Farm Road, Tunbridge Wells, Kent TN2 3DR

Originally published in Italy as *Soutache* by Il Castello Collane
Tecniche, Milano

The author and Publishers would like to thank Filincanto by
Madreperla S.n.c. (Busto Arsizio) and Accessorize (Pavia) for
the materials and Salvatore Ferragamo S.p.A. (Florence) for
granting use of the image on page 9. They would also like
to thank Zodio Italia srl for their help and for the materials
provided for the photographic session at the store in the
Milanofiori-Assago shopping centre.

www.zodio.com

Photography by Studio fotografico Giorgio Uccellini (Milan)

English translation by Burravoe Translation Services

ISBN: 978-1-78221-480-9

Printed in China by 1010 Printing International Ltd.

Donatella Ciotti

SOUTACHE

Search Press

CONTENTS

CREATING WITH SOUTACHE

Jewels have always been a status symbol. The artistry of jewels causes admiration and lends them their attraction; they have often been used as a symbolic display of power and wealth. Over the centuries, people have tried to express their own personalities with jewels, matching timeless stones with precious materials but also using less expensive materials to create the items.

Today, more than ever, there is a demand for these less precious materials, which have thus come into fashion. We are talking about jewellery that in modern-day jargon is known as 'costume jewellery'. It must be made clear that the use of this term is not intended to allude to cheap items found in high-street shops, but to the creations that are appearing more and more frequently on the high-end market, made prestigious by high-fashion brands.

For every expensive material, there is a replica to be found in the world of costume jewellery. For example, rhinestones or crystals imitate diamonds, whilst well-made resin cabochons and glass beads imitate coloured precious stones. Metal can also be plated with gold using a chemical bath. The techniques used to set the stones are identical for both precious jewels and costume jewellery.

In this book I will teach you to make elegant costume jewellery (and much more!) that will enhance anything you wear and help you achieve a truly special look.

First of all, I will introduce you to the basic tools used in soutache jewellery creation, which are easy to source, and inexpensive; we will also explore the various materials that you can use in your projects. Next, I will teach you the basic techniques to use in the projects that follow. In a short time, you will be able to create real 'works of art', and your jewellery box will soon contain elegant rings, shiny pendants to wear as earrings or on chains as necklaces, with matching bracelets that are just as beautiful. You will learn to create brooches that add a touch of class to a simple, elegant dress or hat. The projects in the book also include embellishments for shoes and bags, not to mention hairbands and hair clips that will set off your hairstyles perfectly.

Finally, the book will end with a number of inspirational photographs to further stimulate your creative imagination.

Enjoy the read, and more importantly, enjoy your creations!

Donatella Ciotti

HISTORICAL NOTES

What is soutache flat braid? It is a decorative trim sold in haberdasheries and made in a herringbone weave, and is used to decorate various items. Braided soutache cords are sold in a variety of synthetic and natural materials, including viscose, wool, silk, lurex and cotton. *Soutache* is a French term, used for the first time in the nineteenth century, and comes from the Hungarian word *sujtas*, meaning 'ornamental braid'. *Sujtas*, in fact, was known in the past as a type of *passementerie*, or trim, and used as a decorative technique on clothes, curtains and upholstery.

In France at the end of the nineteenth century, soutache braid was commonly used to decorate shawls and evening gowns. It was also used in France as a sewing technique on high-ranking military uniforms: many decorations in gold soutache can be seen on portraits of Napoleon Bonaparte on his uniform.

Tsars and tsarinas and members of the European military were often depicted wearing dresses and uniforms with soutache decorations. In Spain, gold soutache cord is still used to decorate bullfighters' costumes. It is also used in Italian costume design – we see the use of soutache in the film, *The Leopard*, by Luchino Visconti: the costume designer, Piero Tosi, who worked with Visconti, had a lavish white gown made in etamine for actor Claudia Cardinale, embellished with geometric soutache characteristic of the Second Empire.

Passementerie made using the soutache technique is used as a base for setting stones, to make elegant, high-end jewellery. By combining skilful sewing techniques with soutache it is also possible to create works of art in areas other than jewellery, such as fashion accessories. One such example of soutache in high fashion is the clutch bag by Salvatore Ferragamo, on the opposite page, which was a huge success in his autumn-winter 2012 fashion collection.

Late nineteenth-century French magazines showing dresses decorated using soutache techniques.

Salvatore Ferragamo

MATERIALS:
SOUTACHE CORD

Soutache cord, made from very soft, braided
viscose, is sold in a wide range of colours.

OTHER MATERIALS

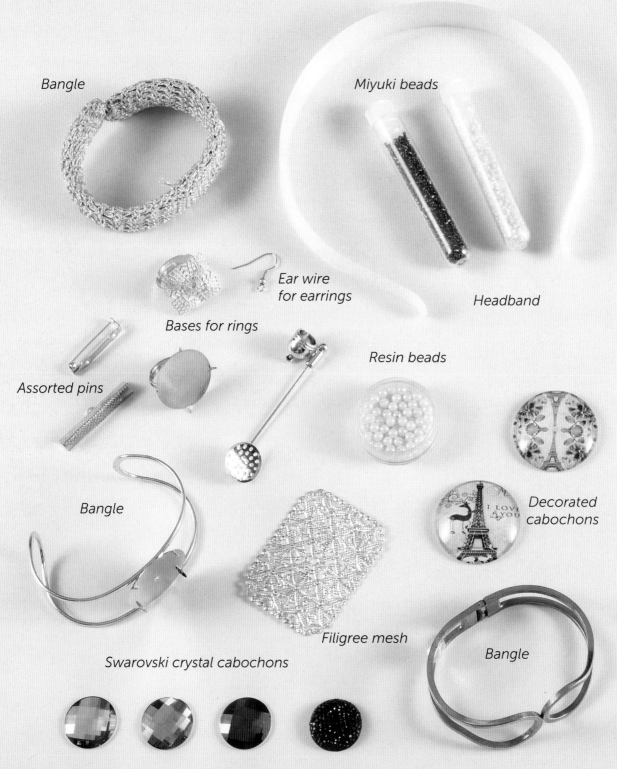

Bangle

Miyuki beads

Ear wire
for earrings

Bases for rings

Headband

Assorted pins

Resin beads

Bangle

Decorated
cabochons

Filigree mesh

Swarovski crystal cabochons

Bangle

Assorted stones

Cardboard coil wrapping rings

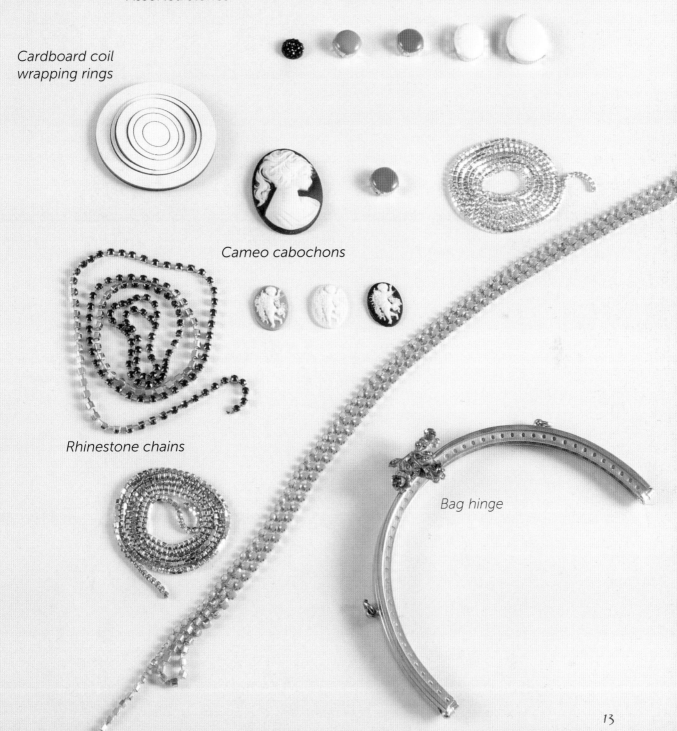

Cameo cabochons

Rhinestone chains

Bag hinge

13

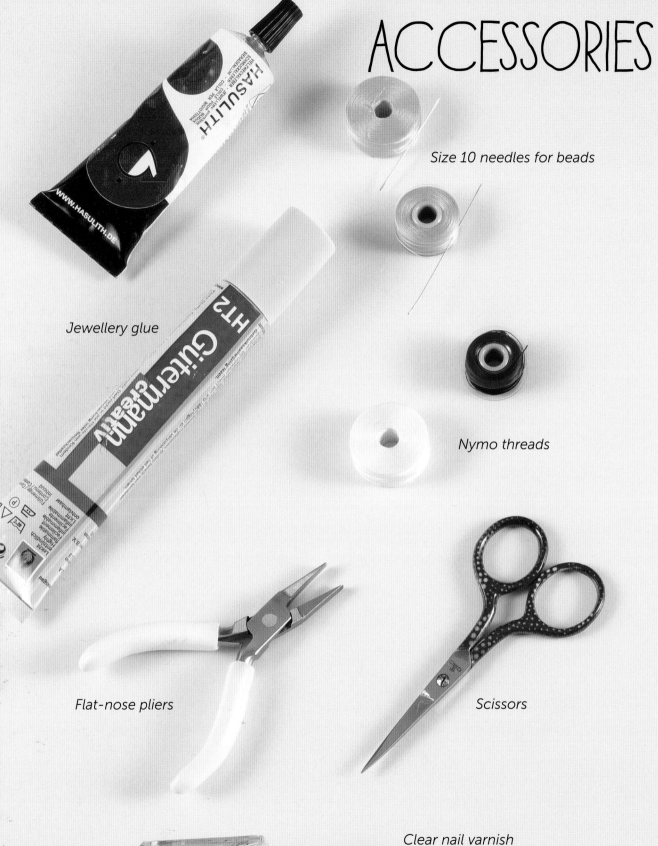

ACCESSORIES

Size 10 needles for beads

Jewellery glue

Nymo threads

Flat-nose pliers

Scissors

Clear nail varnish

Dressmaker's soft measuring tape

Finishing scissors

Alcantara
(covering material)

BEADS AND CRYSTALS

At the centre of the pieces that make up soutache creations are colourful beads, crystals, cabochons and pearls. They may need to be set into a bezel so that they can be sewn to the cords through the holes in the bezel.

PREPARING THE CORDS

1. Soutache cords are braided in a herringbone pattern so can fray at both ends. To solve this problem, paint about 1cm (½in) at each end of the completed braid with a light layer of clear nail varnish.

2. Wait for the varnish to dry then cut about half way along the varnished area (see inset). Repeat the process on the other end and your cord is ready to use.

3. Look closely at a length of cord: it has two raised sides and a central dip. The cord has a rounded, more pronounced part and a thinner, flattened one. When joining cords, they must all face the same way.

> **NOTE**
> It is important that all the lengths of cord are joined together facing in the same direction.

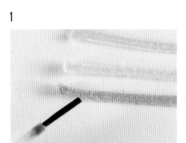

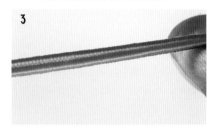

TYING OFF KNOTS

1. Wrap the thread around the needle several times.

2. With your other hand, push the coils closer to the eye of the needle.

3. Remove the needle through the coils to make a knot large enough not to pass through the cord.

4. Pull the thread tight then cut off the ends of the thread after the knot.

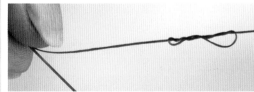

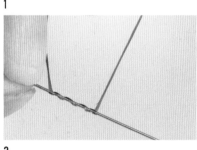

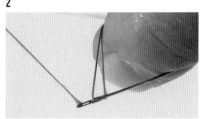

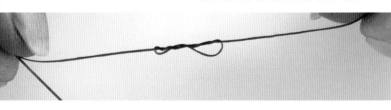

SEWING THE CORDS

1. Take three lengths of cord and place them in layers, flattened firmly against each other. Make a gentle curve with the cords.

2. Hold the cords and insert the needle with the knotted thread through the centre of the curve.

3. Push the needle all the way through. Leave a small gap, then return the needle back to complete the first stitch. Repeat the process on the inner cords only, for a second, almost invisible, stitch.

4. Stitch the entire length of cord in the same way. Do not pull the thread too tightly as this will mark the cord. Similarly, do not leave the thread too loose or the cords will become gappy.

NOTE
Always use thread in the same shade as the cords. A contrasting colour thread has been used in the photographs solely to show the steps to be followed.

1

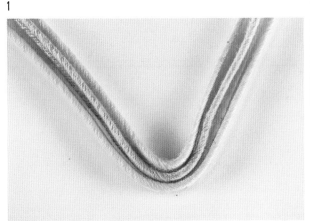

2

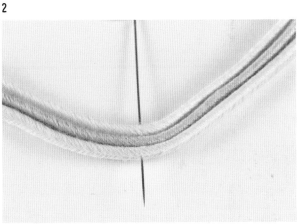

3

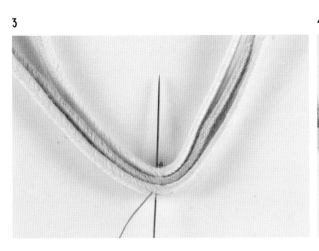

4

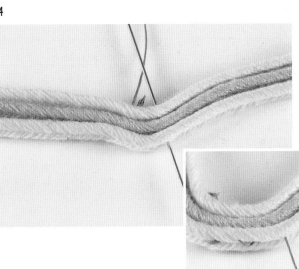

MAKING A BASIC ELEMENT

1. Take three cords, seal the ends and make a few stitches in the centre.

2. Sew small stitches from right to left along the cord for half the circumference of your pearl, creating a slight curve in the cords. This way, the cords will be a smoother shape.

3. Insert the needle through the hole in the pearl and through the three cords on one side of the stitched length. Pull the thread all the way through and mould the cords around the pearl.

4. Move along one stitch and go back into the hole in the pearl. Exit on the other side. In this way the pearl is sewn securely between the cords.

5. Carry on stitching until the cords close around the pearl. Sew the cords together to fully encase the pearl. Secure the work at the point of closure by passing the thread through all the cords several times (see inset).

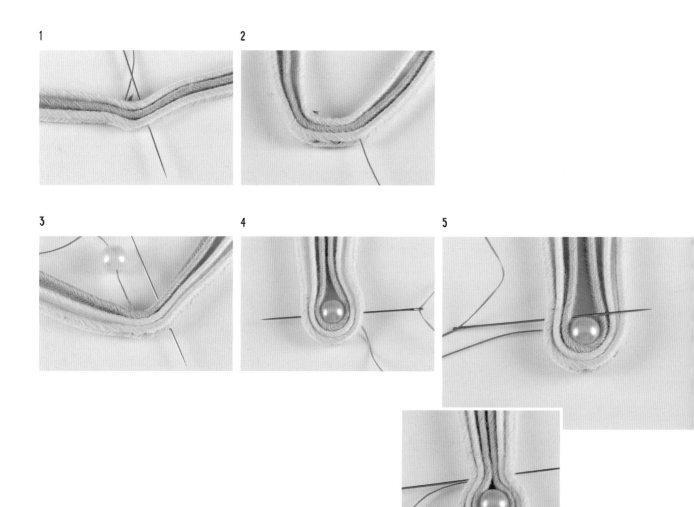

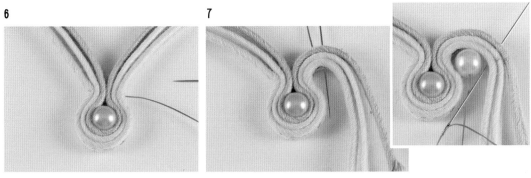

6. With the thread on one side of the work, divide the cord into two groups of three lengths.

7. Make small stitches to create a curve, as in step 2. Thread a pearl into the new curve, and return the needle to the other side through the hole in the pearl. The pearl will now be stitched to the cords (see inset).

8. Turn the piece 180 degrees. Return the needle through the pearl from the outside so the needle passes under the previous pearl. Stitch through the six layers of cord.

9. Stitch the cords as above. Insert a new pearl and stitch back through the pearl and the cords to secure them.

10. Stitch the cords around the pearl and make sure the cord ends are at the back of the piece.

11. Secure the cords on to the back of the piece, folding them slightly to flatten them against the completed work. Stitch the flattened cords to the ones underneath using hidden stitches then tie off with knots.

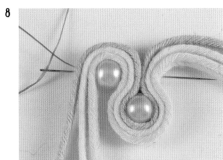

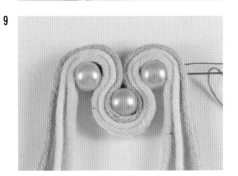

12

13

14

12. Paint a layer of varnish on the ends of the cords and cut off any excess (see inset).

13. You have just made a basic design that can be used for future creations. Look at the finished version, front and back (see inset), in the photographs to see how the piece should look once it is complete.

14. If you want your design to look more elegant, you can finish it around the edges with small beads, embroidered using a brick stitch technique. Make a knot in a length of thread, insert the needle in the back of the design inside the cord (central rib) and pass it to the front.

15. Thread two pearls on to the needle, return it to the back with a stitch, then back to the front. Pass the needle through the hole in the second pearl, from bottom to top. Repeat, inserting another pearl, taking the thread to the back, returning to the front and passing through the hole in the pearl that has just been inserted. Repeat these steps all around the edge of the work.

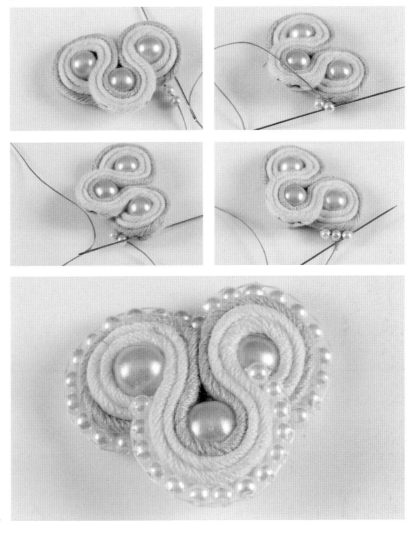

Right, the finished element.

Below, example showing several basic designs used to make a bracelet.

WORKING WITH A CABOCHON

1. Cut a square of Alcantara fabric that is slightly larger than your cabochon. Spread a little jewellery glue on the back of the cabochon and place it on the fabric (inset). Take care that the glue does not seep through the back of the fabric. Wait for the glue to dry before beginning work.

2. For a 30mm (1¼in) diameter cabochon, cut about 20cm (7¾in) of cord, in three colours that complement the colour of your cabochon.

3. Thread a needle and knot the thread. Insert the needle from the back to the front of the material close to the edge of the cabochon.

1

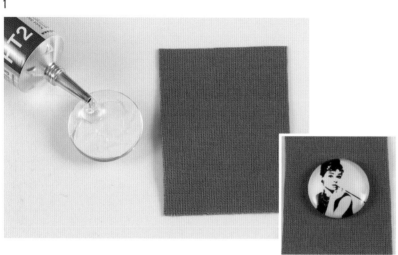

2

3

4. Curve the cords, keeping the lengths equal. Sew the cords together in the centre with a small stitch. Sew the cords to the fabric close to the edge of the cabochon along one side, using small hidden stitches on the front and longer stitches on the back of the fabric (inset).

5. Continue until the cords are sewn all the way around the cabochon. At the bottom of the work there will be six hanging cords. Join the two sets of cords together with a few stitches to complete the circle.

4

5

6. To fill the gap between the two sets of cords, pass the needle through to the inside of one set of three cords, thread a pearl or bead on to the needle so it is positioned in the middle of the cords and pass the needle out through the other cords.

7. Go back through the bead with the needle to make sure the pearl is secure. Sew a few stitches under the pearl to secure it in place.

8. Complete the piece by following the instructions for creating the basic design (see pages 20–23). Take the cords to the back of the piece and sew them to the Alcantara with small stitches. Cut off the excess material.

9. To hide the stitching at the back, cut a piece of Alcantara to fit the back of the piece. Spread jewellery glue on the back of the piece, place it on the Alcantara and press down. Leave it to dry.

10. Cut off the excess Alcantara with sharp scissors.

6

7

8

9

10

SEWING A BEZEL TO THE CORDS

1. Cut three cords about 15cm (6in) long. Take one length and join the two ends. Place a bezel in the curve of the cord. Insert a needle into the hole in the bezel closest to the join of the cord and remove the bezel. Join the other lengths of cord, in line with each other, keeping the knot in the thread inside the cords. Return the bezel to its position, pass the needle through the same hole as before, from the outside inwards and sew along the bezel, entering the next hole from the inside outwards (see inset).

2. Sew the cords together with a small stitch, returning through the bezel hole. Stitch over once more, between the holes to make the work more secure.

3. Once the setting is complete, sew the cords together at the base of the bezel.

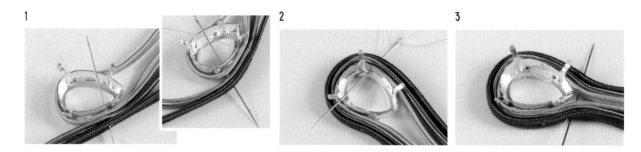

4. Insert a crystal in the bezel. Use flat-nose pliers to close the four prongs on the setting and secure the crystal.

5. Following the basic technique (see pages 20–23), insert a bead between three cords. Pass the needle back through the cords and the hole in the bead to the other side of the work.

6. Insert a bead on the other side in the same way, to form a basic design.

7. Take the thread to the centre on the back of the work and secure the cords with small stitches. Spread a layer of clear nail varnish over the stitches (inset) and cut off the excess lengths of cord.

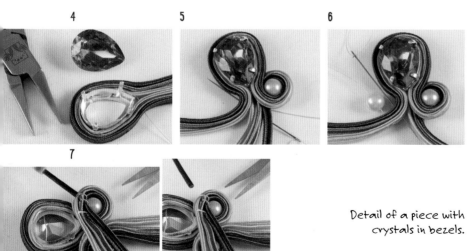

Detail of a piece with crystals in bezels.

SETTING A CABOCHON WITH BEADS

1. Cut an oblong of Alcantara fabric that is slightly larger than your cabochon. Spread a little jewellery glue on the back of the cabochon and fix it to the fabric (see inset).

2. Thread your needle and make a knot. Insert the needle through the back of the fabric and bring it out at the front, close to the top of the cabochon. Thread on two beads and return the needle to the back.

1

2

3. Return the needle to the front of the fabric, passing through the second bead already placed, and insert two new beads onto the thread.

4. Return the needle to the back of the fabric. Continue in this way (see inset) until you have completed the entire perimeter of the cabochon. Fix the thread at the back securely and continue with your chosen design.

3

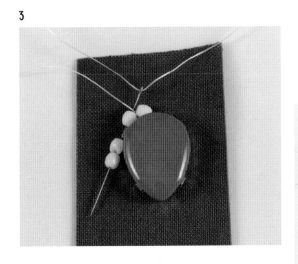

4

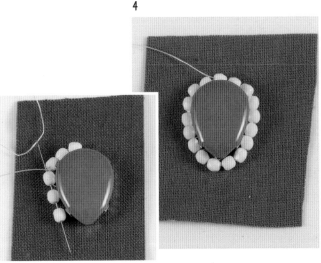

STRIPS WITH BEADS

1. Cut four lengths of cord to the desired length, thread the needle and make a knot. Insert the needle between two cords so that the knot is hidden, thread on a bead and then pass the needle through the other two cords.

2. Draw the two sets of cords together to secure the bead in the middle. Make a small stitch and pass the needle through the cords, the bead and the two opposite cords. Make a small stitch on the front edge of the cord, then return the needle to the back and thread on a new bead. Proceed along the whole length, sewing beads between the cords.

3. Some projects require additional layers to lend a three-dimensional form to the work. In this case, you can create bends with beads. Use the technique described in steps 1 and 2, but when sewing in the beads, curve the cords to the left or the right. keeping the beads straight between the two strips of cord.

1

2

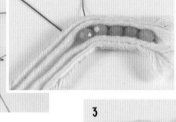

3

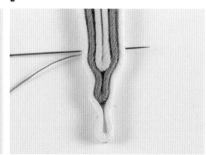

LEAF TECHNIQUE

1. You can create leaves using strips with beads. Cut a length of cord and fold it in half. From the inside, sew two sides of the cord together with a few small stitches to form the tip of the leaf. Fold the second cord in half and insert it inside the first cord as shown. Sew the four layers of cord together with small stitches.

2. Using the same technique, insert another length of cord in the centre of the second and sew all six cords together with small stitches.

1

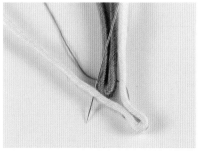

2

ADDING PEARLS TO A LEAF SHAPE

1. With the thread on the inside of the cords, insert a pearl about 1cm (½in) from the last stitch and sew it to the cords. Make sure the pearl is firmly attached to the cords.

2. Continue sewing along the three cords for a short length, then join the six layers of cord together. Continue sewing for the length required.

1

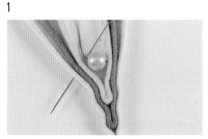

2

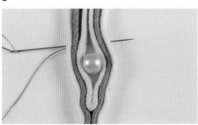

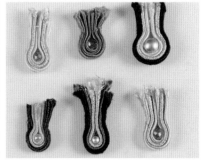

Details of several leaves.

LOZENGE SHAPE LEAF WITH BEADS

1. Repeat the steps for the leaf technique to form the tip of the leaf. Pass the needle through three layers of cords, thread on a bead, sew through the other three cords and then sew through the bead again to secure it.

2. Sew a small stitch and go back through the three cords. Place two more beads in the middle of the cords above the single bead and sew back through the beads to secure them. Insert three more beads above these using the same technique (inset) to increase the width of the leaf.

3. Now carry out the same process in reverse: insert two beads and then one bead, to form a lozenge shape.

4. Sew the six layers of cords together at the base of the beads to create the stem of the leaf. Cut off the excess cord and seal the ends with transparent nail varnish. These leaf details can be made with leftover materials from other projects.

Detail of lozenge shape leaf work.

1

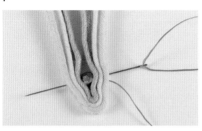

2

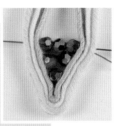

3

4

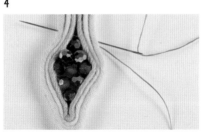

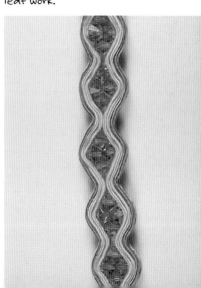

WAVE TECHNIQUE WITH PEARLS

1. Cut six lengths of cord in your choice of colours. Seal the ends with varnish. Sew the six layers together, about 2cm (¾in) along. Secure the two inner cords together with a few stitches.

2. Insert a pearl between the two sets of three cords. Pass the needle through the pearl and through the outer cords. Pass the needle back to secure the pearl in place.

3. Move 1cm (½in) along the cord, making a few stitches as you go.

4. Sew the cords together for 1cm (½in) with a few narrow stitches to form a wave.

5. Separate the cords. On one set of cords only, sew along a length of roughly 1cm (½in), making sure the thread is on the inside at the last stitch. Insert another pearl and pass the needle through the pearl and opposite cords. Go back through the cords and pearl again and through the other cords. Carry on inserting beads along the desired length. To finish, sew together the cords for a length of about 2cm (¾in). Seal the cords.

1

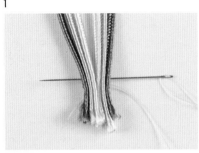

2

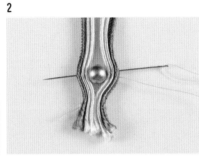

3

4

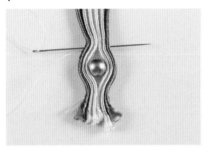

5

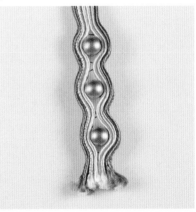

Examples of some of the various techniques described.

WAVE TECHNIQUE WITH SMALL PEARLS AND BEADS

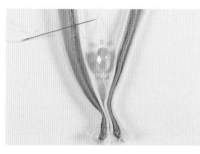

1. Cut six lengths of cord in your colours of choice. Trim the ends after sealing them with nail varnish. Sew the six layers together for about 2cm (¾in). Divide the cords into two groups and sew the first three cords together. Pass the needle to the middle of the cords. Insert a small pearl, an oval bead and another small pearl.

2. Sew the lower pearl to the two inner cords only on either side and secure it in place.

3. Push the needle back up through all the beads.

4. Sew one group of three cords together with small stitches, moving downwards.

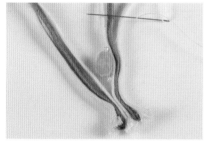

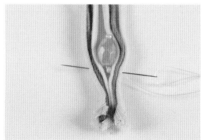

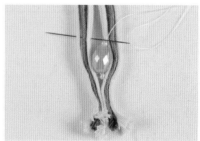

5. Pass the needle back up through the beads and to the other side that has not yet been stitched.

6. Sew along the other side using small stitches and inserting beads as you go. This will create a wave effect with the beads and pearls in the middle of the piece. Secure the six cords together.

7. Repeat the steps above for the length you require.

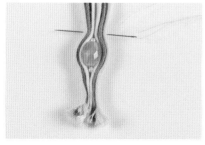

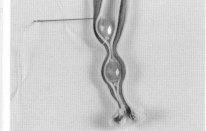

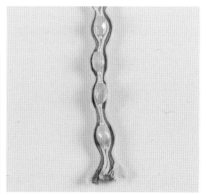

ZIGZAG TECHNIQUE

1. Cut three lengths of cord in the colours of your choice to complement the pearls you are using. Thread the needle and create a knot. Sew the three cords together, leaving about 10cm (4in) unsewn at each end.

2. Curve the cords in the centre, insert the first pearl and, using the basic technique on pages 20–23, secure the pearl between the cords. Carry on sewing around the pearl and then make a few stitches at the base to secure the pearl in place (inset).

1

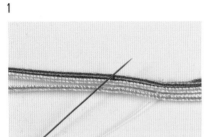

2

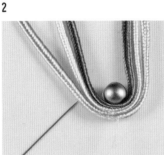 

3. Curve three of the cords back on themselves and secure in place using small stitches. Insert another pearl and sew it to the cords.

4. Return the needle through the cords, through the second pearl and through the other three cords. Sew the cords at the bend and return the thread to the direction of the work.

3

4

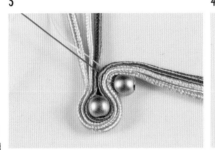

5. Carry on sewing until the pearl is completely enclosed by the cords and secure the six layers of cord. Fold the cords again, secure with stitches and insert a pearl to form another curve.

6. Using the wave technique on pages 30–31, insert a bead as an added embellishment.

7. Continue the technique along the length of cord to achieve the desired zigzag effect.

5

6

7

NOTE
Using the same technique, you can work with cords in grosgrain.

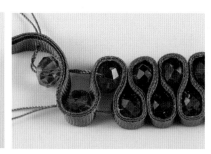

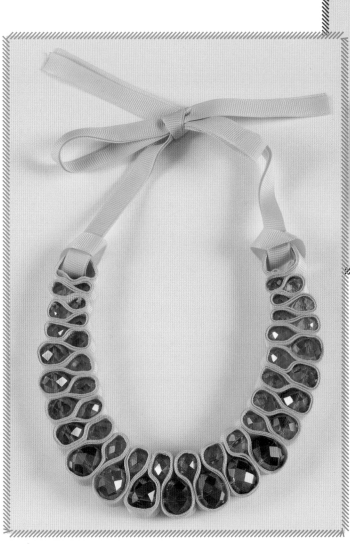

Finished items.

33

COIL TECHNIQUE

1. Cut a single cord to 50cm (19¾in) in length and seal the ends with varnish to prevent them fraying during the coiling process. Fold the cord back on itself, leaving about 2cm (¾in) of cord hanging at one end. Thread the needle with thread the same colour as the cord and make the knot. Make a first stitch, then wrap the cord round itself in a circle. Next, sew the circle together from the outside in to secure the work (inset).

2. Coil the cord around itself again and secure the work at various points, from the outside in.

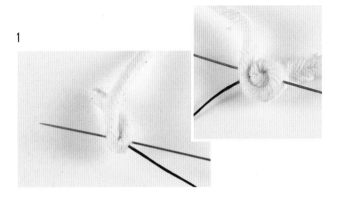

1

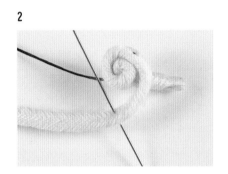

2

3. Continue to coil the cord around itself several times and stitch several times to secure it. Turn the work over and stitch the coils with diagonal stitches so that they do not move out of place. Continue in this way until the piece reaches the required size.

4. Once your coil is complete, sew the ends of the cord firmly to the back of the piece (two examples of this process are shown below). Spread a layer of varnish on the ends to prevent the cord from fraying. Cut off any excess.

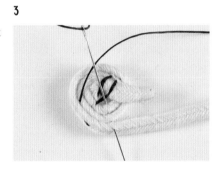

3

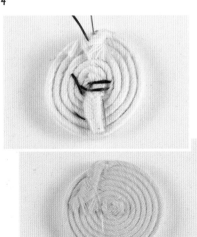

4

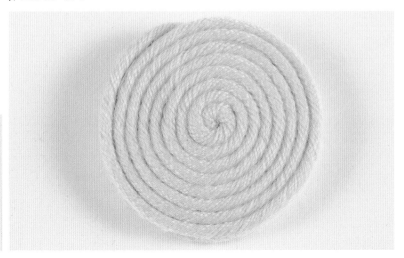

A finished coil.

COIL WITH A PEARL

1. Cut a length of cord of about 50cm (19¾in), insert the needle with the knot about 3cm (1¼in) from the beginning, then pass the needle through the middle of the cord to create a curve. Place a pearl inside the curve. Pass the needle through the pearl (inset). Wrap the cord around the pearl two or three times to form a coil and secure in place with stitches.

2. Carry on wrapping the cord around the pearl, sewing long stitches on the outside every time you make a full circle. When finished, stitch the cords to secure.

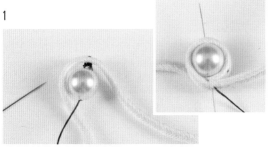

1

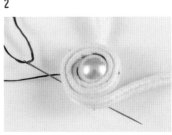

2

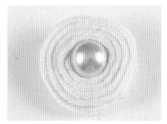

DOUBLE COLOUR COILS

1. Cut two lengths of cord in contrasting colours. Bend the cords in half, secure with a stitch in the centre and sew a few stitches to form a tip. This will be the middle of the work.

2. Coil the cords around themselves, starting from the middle. Form a small coil and secure in place.

3. Pass the needle through from one side of the coil to the other. Wrap a little of the coil around the middle at a time and sew the coil in place to secure it as you go. The cords must be tight and compact and keep the coil flat and even.

4. Continue to coil until you reach the required size. As you coil, sew long stitches on the outside cord to secure the piece as they will be hidden in the next rotation.

5. When finished, take the end of the cords to the back of the piece and secure them to stop your coil unravelling.

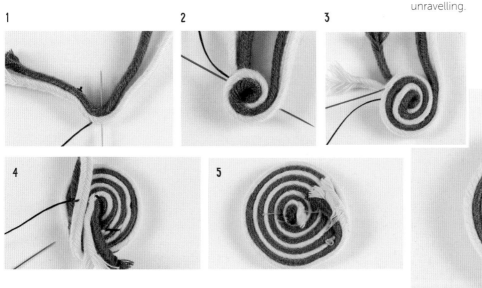

SPIRAL BUTTONS

1. Cut a length of about 15cm (6in) of cord in the colour of your choice. Thread the needle with matching coloured thread and make a knot. Fold the cord back on itself for about 0.5cm (¼in) and stitch it, keeping the fold on the inside. Wrap once and sew with small stitches (inset).

2. After wrapping a couple of times, insert a pencil tip into the middle. As you continue to wrap around the pencil tip, sew small stitches to secure the coils. At the same time, press the work slightly outwards, making a cone shape around the pencil tip. Remove the pencil.

1

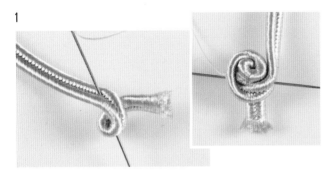

2

3

3. Turn the cord towards the outside to make a small angle and secure with a stitch. Carry on wrapping and bending to form petals.

4. Once you have the desired shape and size, cut the cord and sew the ends on the back of the piece.

4

5

5. Spread a little jewellery glue on the concave part of a button back. Press the button on to the back lightly, making sure it sticks to the base (inset).

Completed rose-shaped spiral buttons.

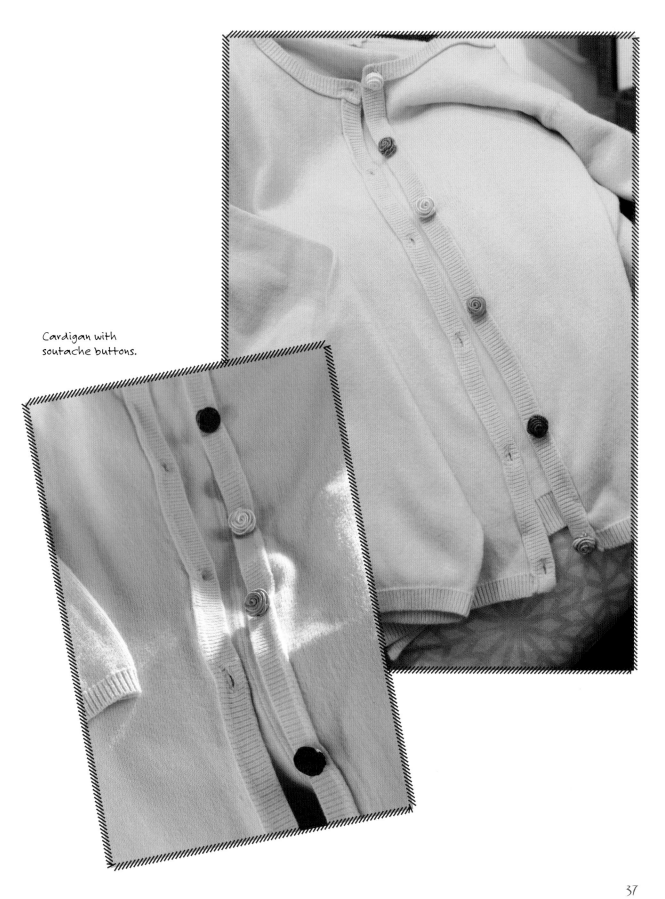

Cardigan with
soutache buttons.

COIL WRAPPING
ON RINGS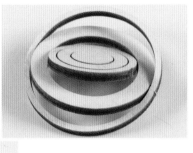

1. Buy a set of coil wrapping rings and choose the size you want, or make one yourself from thick cardboard.

2. Cut a length of cord in the colour of your choice and glue one end of the cord to the back of the cardboard.

1

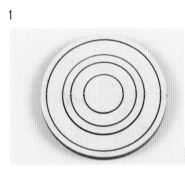

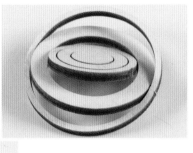

2

3. Wrap the cord around the ring evenly. As the inside of the round is smaller make sure the wraps are close together, using your nail to push them into place.

3

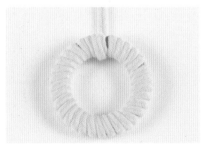

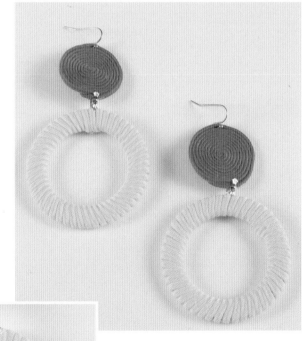

4. When the ring is covered, glue the end of the cord next to the starting point. Cut off the excess cord and seal the end with a layer of clear varnish.

4

Above and opposite, earrings created using the coil technique and coil wrapping on rings.

SEWING RHINESTONE CHAINS TO THE CORDS 🌀

1. Cut three cords. Fold two cords in half so that they are equal lengths and sew them together in the centre of the curve with small stitches. Attach a drop crystal to the cords through the holes in the bezel (see page 26).

Insert a small bead at the base of the bezel (inset). Sew the four inner cords together, passing the needle through the bead to secure everything in place.

2. Pass the needle to one side of the work. Make a loop with the thread and wrap this tightly around the chain between the first and second rhinestones, to secure the chain to the cords.

1

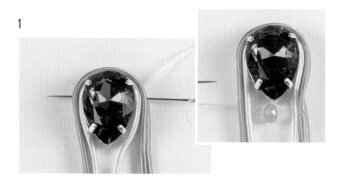

2

3. Pass the needle through the cords to make a second loop on the opposite side. Curve the chain along the cords around the outside of the drop crystal and insert it into the new loop. You now have two choices: you can make the chain slightly taut to open up the rhinestones into a fan shape or you can keep the rhinestones close together. In both cases, secure the chain with a new loop and cut off the excess after the first rhinestone that falls outside the loop. Tie the chain to the cord with a second loop to ensure it is secure.

4. Sew the chain to the cords, using hidden stitches between the rhinestones along the full length of the chain. Make sure the chain is facing forwards.

3

4

5

6

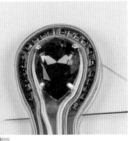

5. Place the third cord at the centre of the work at the top. Pass the needles to the front of the work.

6. Sew the top cord to the chain, stitching in the spaces between the rhinestones from the top to the bottom of the chain. Repeat on the other side, starting from the top of the piece and working down. Join the six cords with a few stitches at the base (inset) and secure the thread on the back. Cut off the excess.

> **NOTE**
> You can also sew link chains on to soutache cord using this technique, as seen below. The chains must be flat and the ends of the links must be tightly secured.

SEWING BEADS AROUND A CABOCHON

1a. To fit a large, round cabochon, cut about 1.5 metres (5ft) of thread. Thread on 34 beads in one colour (pink). Move them about 20cm (7¼in) from the start of the thread, tie them into a circle and secure with a double knot. This is your base circle.

• For the 1st round, thread on a pale pink bead so it sits next to a bead on the base circle and sticks out. Skip one bead on the base circle, then thread through the next bead on the base circle. Next, thread on another pink bead that sticks out from the base circle. Repeat all the way around the base circle.

• At the end of the 1st round, pass the needle through one bead from the previous – base – circle and the 1st bead on the 1st round. Do this at the end of every round.

• To make the 2nd round, thread on a bead in a different colour (fuchsia). Skip one 1st-round bead and thread the needle through the next 1st-round bead that sticks out. Then thread on another fuchsia (2nd-round), bead. Carry on all the way round.

• Work the 3rd round as per the 2nd, with fuchsia beads.

1a

1b

2a

2b

2a. Insert the cabochon into the work. For the 4th round, thread on a fuchsia bead, skip a bead on the 3rd round, and pass the needle through the next two protruding beads on the 3rd round. Continue all the way round.

2b. At the 5th round, thread on a fuchsia bead, then pass the needle through the next protruding 4th-round bead. Thread on another bead on the 5th round. Complete the whole round in this way and repeat for the 6th and 7th (final) rounds, all in fuchsia.

3

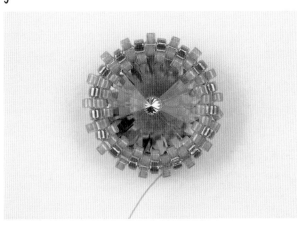

3. Pass the thread between the beads to emerge from a bead on the 2nd round. Thread on a fuchsia bead and pass the needle through the next bead on the 2nd round. Continue all the way round. Work another round in the same way with the beads in the 3rd round, this time threading on pale pink beads. Only trim off the thread if you do not want to sew beads around a second cabochon.

4

4. To wrap an oval cabochon, cut a piece of thread about 1.5 metres (5ft) long and thread the needle. Thread 40 beads in one colour (dark blue), move them to about 20cm (7¾in) from the beginning of the thread and make a base circle as in step 1a on page 42. Tie the circle with a knot and then a double knot. Thread on the rounds of beads in the same way as for the large, round cabochon, from the 1st to the 7th round, switching to pale blue beads at the 2nd round.

5

5. Pass the thread between the beads to emerge from a dark blue bead on the 1st round. Work the beads on this round as for the large round cabochon, following step 3, above, to complete the wrapping.

6. Return to your original piece from pages 42–43. Thread the needle back through one of the beads sticking out on the 2nd round. Thread on a pink bead, then a fuchsia bead, and another pink bead, then thread the needle through another bead on the 2nd round that is sticking out. Let the thread slacken slightly, then thread on a fuchsia bead, a crystal and then another fuchsia bead. Thread the needle back through the crystal to make a loop (skipping the fuchsia bead just threaded). Return the needle to the central motif and thread through the closest bead that is sticking out. Thread on another pink bead, a fuchsia bead, a pink bead and another fuchsia bead, and end that round with a pink bead. Then thread through the next bead sticking out and tie off the thread.

Use the loop to make the beaded motif into a hanging decoration. Decorate the purple oval cabochon in the same way.

6

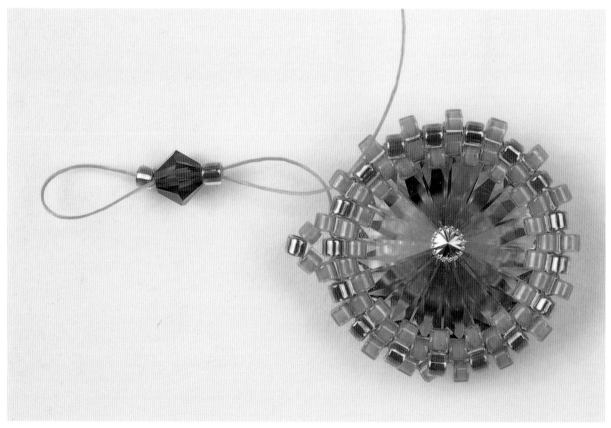

SEWING CORD TO A BEADED CABOCHON

1

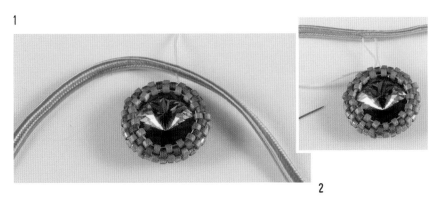

1. Cut a length of soutache cord and varnish the ends. Thread the needle and make a knot. Pass the needle through the middle of the cord, to the back and through the hole in a protruding bead (inset).

2. Pass the needle to the front of the cord with a small stitch, then return to the back, pass through another protruding bead and back to the front. Continue like this to stitch all the protruding beads to the cord.

2

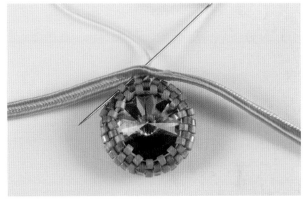

3. When this is done, cut another length of cord. Trim the ends and then sew the new cord on to the one already sewn to the cabochon.

3

GLUING TECHNIQUE

1. Cut a length of cord and varnish the ends. Take the stone or cabochon that you wish to use and place a drop of jewellery glue at one point on the edge. Stick the stone to the middle of the cord so that the cord is an even length on both sides (inset).

2. Put a little more glue on the edge of the stone. Use a toothpick to do this as too much glue will make the cord slide and make the work dirty. Wait a moment, then press the cord around the edge of the stone. Stick it well, pressing down slightly.

3. Continue to apply the cord around the cabochon until it has been completely glued. Take care that the glue does not get on the front of the stone as it is not easy to remove once it has dried. The first round will then be complete.

4

4. For the second round, cut a new length of cord and trim the ends. Apply a drop of glue to the cord that is already glued in place and place the new length over it so that the glue cannot be seen from the front. Continue like this until the second cord is stuck down (inset). Stick small areas at a time so that your fingers do not come into contact with the glue. Use the same technique to glue any other cords that you wish to apply.

NOTE:
Wet glue can be removed from fingers by washing hands with soap and water. If the glue has dried, remove with nail varnish remover. Glue on fabric cannot be removed, however, so be careful.

5

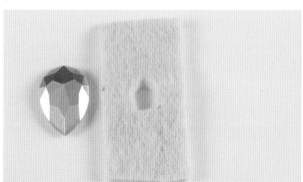

5. To glue a multi-faceted crystal without a flat bottom, cut out a piece of felt bigger than the crystal.

6

6. Cut a hole in it the depth of the crystal and the size of the bottom-most 'face' of the crystal, to hold it. Glue the rear of the crystal to the felt.

BRACELETS

WAVE BRACELET

Materials

* 75CM (29½IN) SOUTACHE CORD IN APRICOT, BROWN AND METALLIC ORANGE
* 17 6MM (¼IN) DIAMETER BICONE SWAROVSKI CRYSTALS
* 3 10MM (½IN) DIAMETER BICONE SWAROVSKI CRYSTALS
* MATCHING NYMO THREAD
* 1 BEADING NEEDLE NO. 10
* 2CM (¾IN) HOOK AND LOOP FASTENER
* SCISSORS

1. Cut three 30cm (11¾in) sets of lengths from the three cords. Varnish the ends and leave them to dry.

2. Thread the needle with thread and make a knot. Bring three of the cords together starting with the brown cord, then the metallic orange one and then the apricot one. Level the ends at one end. Pass the needle between the cords so that the knot is hidden inside the work. Sew together with a stitch. Take the other three cords and sew the brown, metallic and apricot ones to the first ones in that order (inset). Keep them flat against each other.

1

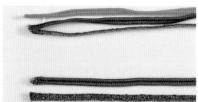

2

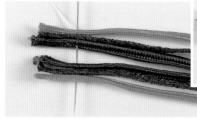

3. Continue sewing for 2cm (¼in), making small stitches on the outside and longer on the inside. Divide the cords into two groups of three again, and sew one set together with a few stitches.

4. Pass the needle to the inside and insert a 6mm (¼in) crystal.

5. Sew all the cords together following the crystal, to secure the crystal in place.

6. Continue sewing the cords and inserting crystals for the desired length. When finished, trim the ends and seal with a layer of glue.

7. With the three remaining 15cm (6in) lengths, create a basic element (see pages 20–23) as a fastener for the bracelet. Sew the piece to the bracelet with hidden stitches.

8. Cut 1cm (½in) of hook and loop fastener. Place one piece on the end of the bracelet and one on the back of the basic element so they act as the bracelet fastening, and trim any excess.

3

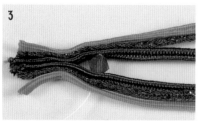

4

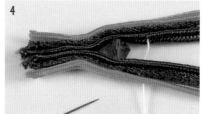

5

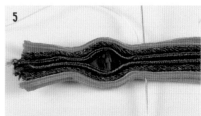

6

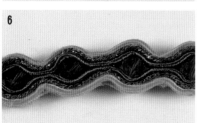

7

8

ZIGZAG BRACELET

Materials

* 1M (3FT) OF SOUTACHE CORD IN FUCHSIA, MAGENTA AND BURGUNDY
* 26 PINK 8MM (¼IN) DIAMETER PINK SWAROVSKI PEARLS
* 24 3MM DIAMETER PINK BEADS
* 1 CLOSED RING
* 1 SPRING CLASP
* 20CM (7¾IN) BURGUNDY RIBBON
* JEWELLERY GLUE
* BEADING NEEDLE NO. 10
* MATCHING NYMO THREAD

1. Seal the ends of the cords with nail varnish. Cut about 50cm (19¾in) of thread, thread the needle and make the knot. Join the fuchsia, magenta and burgundy cords. Stitch the three cords together 5cm (2in) from the start, then make a few small stitches on the front. Pass the needle to the inside of the cords and thread on a pearl (inset).

2. Pass the needle through the three cords on the opposite side and fold the cords around the pearl. A few millimetres (¼in) further on, pass the needle back through the cords, into the pearl and out the other side. Stitch up to the base. Pass the needle through the cords on one side, thread on a small pearl and come out on the opposite side. Repeat to secure the work.

1

2

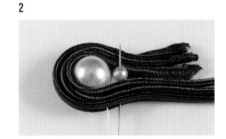

3. Sew the cords together with small stitches to create another curve. Insert a new pearl. Sew the pearl between the cords as in step 1 (inset). Repeat the same steps until you reach the desired length.

4. On completion seal the cords by spreading on a light layer of jewellery glue.

3

4

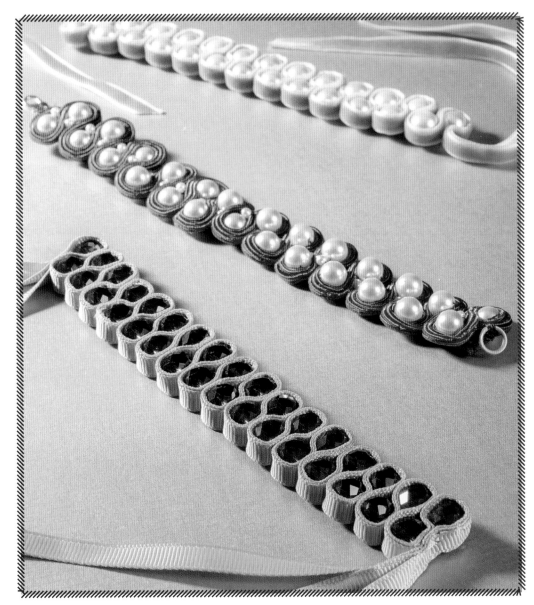

5. Sew the spring clasp on to one end with matching coloured thread and the closed ring on the other side (see inset).

6. Spread jewellery glue on the ribbon then fix it to the back of the piece to hide any knots, and glue.

Above, the same model has been made in two different versions: grosgrain with Swarovski crystals, and velvet with pearls.

5

6

MULTICOLOUR BRACELET

1. Cut the cords in half and seal the two ends with varnish. Position the cords on a macramé support in the following order from right to left: cream, lilac, lime green, pea green, cream, pea green, lilac, lime green, light purple, dark purple, dark purple, light purple. Trim at one end, stick the cords to the support with glue and then pin them in place securely.

2. Weave the first length of cream cord diagonally to the left to form the warp. The warp will pass over the first lilac cord, under the lime green, over the pea green, under the cream, over the pea green, under the lilac, over the lime green, under the light purple, over the dark purple, under the dark purple and over the light purple.

3. Still working from right to left, weave the second (lilac) cord, in the same way, starting by going under the lime green cord.

Materials

* 50CM (19¾IN) OF SOUTACHE CORD IN LIME GREEN, PEA GREEN, CREAM, LIGHT PURPLE AND DARK PURPLE
* 25CM (9¾IN) OF LILAC CORD
* 2 3.5CM (9IN) HOOK CLASPS
* 2 OPEN RINGS
* 1 SPRING CLASP
* FASTENING RING
* SCISSORS
* PINS
* JEWELLERY GLUE
* 1 FLAT MACRAMÉ SUPPORT
* MATCHING NYMO THREAD

1

2

3

4. At the end of each step, weave in the cord from the previous step so that this is the last cord on the weave. Keep the cords flat even when you create the curves on both sides.

5. Continue the work for the required length. At the end of the work, secure the weave with pins.

6. Using matching thread, sew the cords to each other, to secure them. Keep the work flat while sewing.

4

5

6

7. Cut off the excess cords on both ends and varnish the ends. When the varnish is dry, strengthen both ends with a little jewellery glue. Insert each end into a hook clasp, taking care that the cord ends are pushed well inside. Press the clasp sides together with pliers (inset).

8. Complete the bracelet by attaching two open rings to the spring clasp at one end and the fastening ring to the other end.

7

8

TWO-COLOUR PLAITED BRACELET

Materials

* 60CM (23½IN) SOUTACHE CORD IN ORANGE AND LIME GREEN
* MATCHING NYMO THREAD
* 2 CAP ENDS
* 1 OPEN RING
* 1 SPRING CLASP
* SCISSORS
* 3 CHARMS OF YOUR CHOICE
* JEWELLERY GLUE

1. Take the cords and seal the ends with varnish. Create a loop at the end of each of the two cords and sew in place with small stitches. Insert the orange loop inside the green one (see inset).

2. Make a second loop with the green cord. Insert the first green loop into the orange loop. Tighten the orange cord so it fits around the green one. Make a second loop with the orange cord and insert it into the second green loop. Tighten the loops.

1

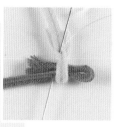

2

3. Continue in this way, alternating the colours. Always loop the cords in the same direction.

4. Make sure the loops form a regular and even-sized plait.

3

4

5. To finish, insert a single cord inside the last loop and pull it tight, like a noose. Spread on a drop of glue and repeat on the other cord. Cut off the excess cord. Place jewellery glue inside a cap end and place it on the end of the plaited cord, pressing down lightly to fix it in position. Repeat on the other end. Hook the spring clasp and charms on to the open ring and attach it to one end of the bracelet.

RINGS

PINK RING WITH CABOCHON

Materials

* 40CM (15¾IN) SOUTACHE CORD IN PINK, METALLIC PINK AND DARK PINK
* 1 CAMEO CABOCHON
* 10 X 10 CM (4 X 4IN) ALCANTARA
* 2 10MM (½IN) DIAMETER ROUND PINK SWAROVSKI CRYSTALS
* 2 10MM (½IN) DIAMETER PINK CRYSTAL SPHERE
* 10CM (4IN) PINK RHINESTONE CHAIN
* MATCHING NYMO THREAD
* 1 RING BASE
* SCISSORS
* JEWELLERY GLUE
* NYMO THREAD
* BEADING NEEDLE

1. Cut out a rectangle of Alcantara that is larger than your cameo. Spread jewellery glue on the back of the cameo (inset 1b), taking care that it does not spread around the sides, and place the cameo on the fabric (inset 1c).

1a

1b

1c
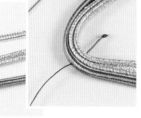

2
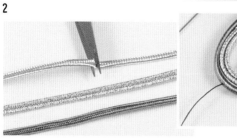

2. Cut the three cords in half and seal the ends with varnish. Join one set of three cords in the following order from right to left: metallic pink, pink and dark pink. Make sure the ends are level. Thread the needle, make the knot and sew a stitch in the middle of the cords from the inside out (inset). Do the same with the second set of cords.

3. Position both sets of cords so the cameo is between them. Make sure there is a metallic pink cord next to the cameo on both sides.

4. On one side, sew the cords to the Alcantara, from the centre upwards, with small stitches on the front and longer stitches on the back. When you reach the top of the cameo stop sewing but do not cut the cords. Return the needle to the centre of the work, and repeat from the centre downwards.

5. Secure the thread when finished and sew the cords on the other side in the same way.

6. Trim the excess fabric around the cords.

3
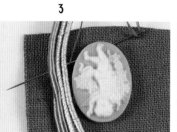

4

5

6
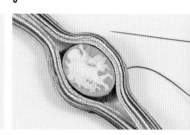

7. Join the two sets of cords together at the base of the cameo with a few stitches. Divide the cords into two sets, curve them away from the join and attach the pink crystals using the technique described on page 21 (inset). Repeat at the other end of the cabochon.

7

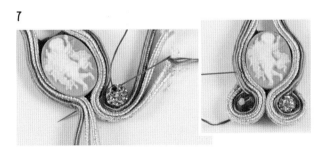

8

9

8. Cut 3cm (1¼in) of rhinestone chain and sew it in place to the left of the cabochon between the coils. Repeat on the right-hand side.

9. Spread a layer of jewellery glue on the back of the work and fix it to the ring base.

The finished ring.

LIME GREEN AND LILAC RING

Materials

* 50CM (19¾IN) SOUTACHE CORD IN DARK LILAC
* 10CM (4IN) SOUTACHE CORD IN LIGHT LILAC
* 15CM (6IN) SOUTACHE CORD IN LIGHT GREEN AND LIME GREEN
* 1 LIGHT GREEN SWAROVSKI CRYSTAL WITH 8MM (¼IN) DIAMETER BEZEL
* 2 6MM (¼IN) DIAMETER LILAC BICONE CRYSTALS
* 1 8MM (¼IN) DIAMETER PINK PEARL
* 2 3MM DIAMETER BEADS
* 15CM (6IN) PINK RHINESTONE CHAIN
* 1 RING BASE
* 10 X 10CM (4 X 4IN) ALCANTARA IN MATCHING COLOUR
* MATCHING NYMO THREAD
* SCISSORS
* CLIPPERS

1. Cut two lengths of 15cm (6in) from the dark lilac cord. Varnish the ends of the cords. Then set them aside. Curve the two 15cm (6in) lengths of green cord so that one side is 5cm (2in) long. Place a green crystal in the curve and begin to stitch.

2. Hold the cord tight around the crystal and sew the crystal to the cords through the holes.

3. Line up the two dark lilac cords with the green cord, leaving an extra 5cm (2in) on the same side (inset). Sew all the cords together to the base of the crystal (see inset).

1

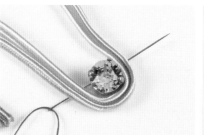

2

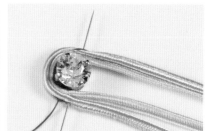

3

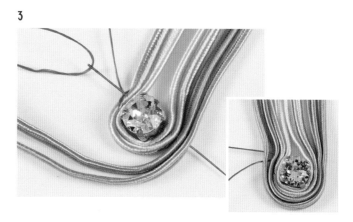

4

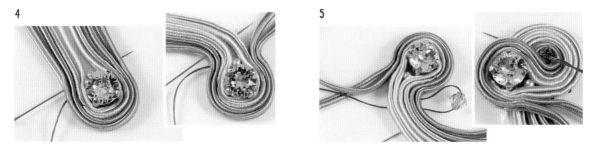

5

4. Insert a small bead at the base of the crystal between the two sets of cords and sew the eight cords together (inset) taking care to secure the bead in position.

5. Sew the four green cords to the two lilac ones on the right hand side, curve to the left and make a few stitches to secure the six cords. Insert a bicone crystal and sew the six cords around it. At the end, place the six cords at the back of the work and secure with small stitches (inset). Cut off the excess but do not throw away the leftover parts.

6

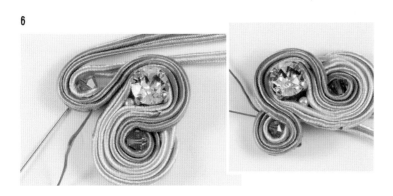

6. On the other side, sew the two dark lilac cords from step 1 together, curving them slightly. Position the leftover green cord in the middle and sew the three cords together. Insert a bicone crystal. Secure with a few stitches through the crystal and the cords. Secure all loose ends at the back of the piece (see inset).

7

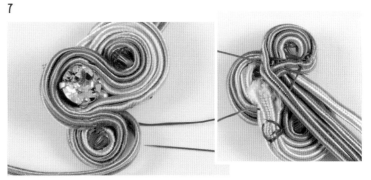

7. Cut another 5cm (2in) of dark lilac cord and sew this length to the curve of dark lilac on the left of the piece. When this is done, take the cords to the back of the piece, secure with small stitches (inset) and trim off the excess.

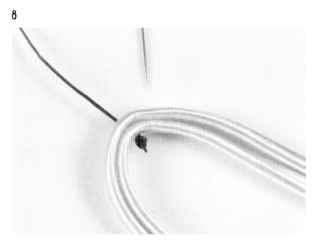

8. Bend the light lilac cord in half to make a curve and sew a few stitches in the middle to secure it.

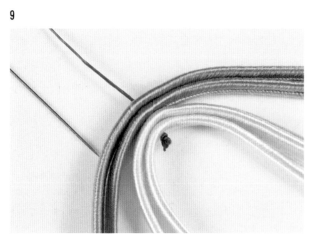

9. Sew the remaining dark lilac cords over the curve and sew along for about 5mm (¼in).

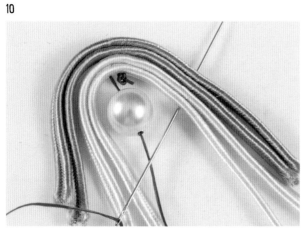

10. Thread on the pink pearl. Pass the needle back from the outside inwards through the pearl. Join the cords at the base of the pearl and stitch together for a few millimetres (¼in). Cut off the excess cords and spread a layer of varnish on the ends. Secure all the ends to the back of the piece.

11. Attach the rhinestone chain on the upper part and lower part of the piece (following the instructions on page 40).

12. Cut a square of Alcantara. Spread a layer of glue on the back of the piece and press it down on the fabric. Make sure it sticks well. Cut off any excess fabric around the motif, Using the jewellery glue, stick the piece on to the base of the ring.

11

12

The finished ring.

PINK AND TURQUOISE RING

1. Double up the pink cord, cut it in half and seal the ends with varnish. Thread the needle and make a knot. Curve the two cords together to form equal lengths and sew in the middle for 0.5cm (¼in) from the inside outwards with small stitches. Insert the pink crystal and curve the cords around it. Sew the four cords together at the base of the pink crystal (inset).

2. On the left of the crystal, form the cords into a curve and place a pearl in the curve. Pass the needle through to the inside of the cords a little way down from the pearl. Thread on the pearl and pass the needle back diagonally through all four cords, higher up the cords so that the stitch pulls the cords around the pearl.

Materials

* 20CM (7¾IN) SOUTACHE CORD IN METALLIC PINK
* 10CM (4IN) SOUTACHE CORD IN LIGHT BLUE, TURQUOISE, BOTTLE GREEN AND LIME GREEN
* 1 10MM (½IN) DIAMETER PINK CRYSTAL SPHERE
* 2 8MM (¼IN) DIAMETER PINK PEARLS
* 1 8MM (¼IN) DIAMETER BLUE BRIOLETTE CRYSTAL
* 10CM (4IN) TURQUOISE RHINESTONE CHAIN
* 1 RING BASE
* BEADING NEEDLE NO. 10
* MATCHING NYMO THREAD
* 10 X 10CM (4 X 4IN) ALCANTARA IN MATCHING COLOUR
* SCISSORS
* JEWELLERY GLUE

1

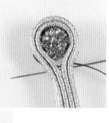

2

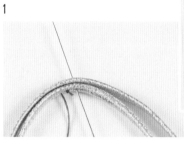

3

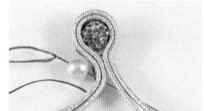 

3. Pass the needle back through the pearl and the four cords so that it is on the opposite side. Insert the right-hand pearl in the same way. Insert the pearl, sew the cords around the pearl and secure the ends to the back of the piece with a few stitches (inset).

4. Cut the lime green cord in two, double up both lengths and sew one end together with small stitches.

5. Curve the double cord around the right-hand pearl. Secure the ends of the green cords to the back of the

piece and sew it on to the work with small stitches. There should now be four rounds of cord around the right-hand pearl.

6. Secure the cord ends to the back of the work.

4

5

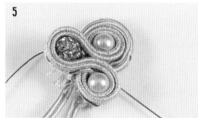

6

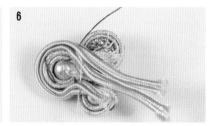

7. Sew the light blue and turquoise cords together for about 5cm (2in), creating a slight curve. Do not cut the excess cord. Sew the rhinestone chain on to the curve against the turquoise cord (see inset).

8. Sew the green cord on to the chain from the beginning of the length for about 5cm (2in). Secure with stitches through all the cords. At the non-chain end, curve the cords around the blue briolette crystal (inset). Secure the loose ends at the back.

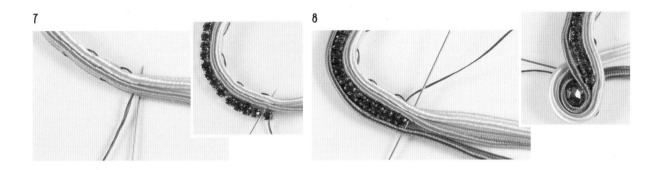

9. Place the blue piece next to the pink crystal on the left-hand side as shown and secure with glue.

10. Spread a layer of glue on the back of the work and press it gently on to the Alcantara. Leave to dry then cut off the excess fabric. Spread a little glue on to the ring base and fix the finished piece on it (inset). Leave to dry.

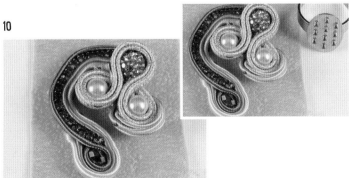

The finished ring.

HEADBANDS

GREEN HEADBAND

1. Apply the double-sided adhesive tape inside and outside the headband.

1

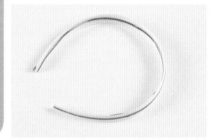

2. Wrap the ribbon round the headband. Starting from one end, remove the protective paper from the adhesive tape as you wrap the ribbon round the headband. Keep the ribbon straight and wrap it evenly, making sure each wrap of ribbon is next to the previous one without overlapping it (inset 2b). End the last wrap inside the headband and cut off the excess ribbon (inset 2c). Fold the ribbon under to make a small hem and secure it with a drop of glue.

3. Glue the cabochon on to the Alcantara and wait for it to dry. Cut six 25cm (9¾in) lengths from the cords and seal the ends with varnish.

2a

3

4. Thread the needle and tie a knot. Sew the metallic green and fuchsia cords around the cabochon (see pages 24–25) to cover one edge of the cabochon, leaving about 10cm (4in) of cord free at either end.

5. Position the rhinestone chain on the fuchsia cord and sew it to all the cords and Alcantara fabric, between the rhinestones, When the length has been completed cut off the excess chain (but not the cords).

6. Position the apple-green cord along the rhinestone chain, leaving about 10cm (4in) free at both ends. Sew the cord on to the chain. Repeat steps 4, 5 and 6 on the other side. Cut off the excess Alcantara. Stitch together the six cords at the base of the cabochon (inset).

4

5

6

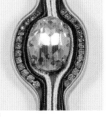

7. Divide the six cords into two sets. Sew one set together, curving them to the left.

8. Position a fuchsia pearl in the curve. Pass the needle back through the pearl and cords then stitch to secure the pearl in place.

9. Sew a few more stitches along, curve the cords to the left, insert a green crystal, then pass the needle back through the crystal and the cords. Secure the cords to the back of the piece.

10. Repeat the steps described above on the top part of the same side, inserting another fuchsia pearl and a fuchsia olive pearl to complete the first half of the piece. Repeat on the other side in a mirror image.

7

8

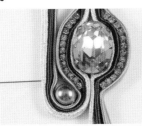

9

10

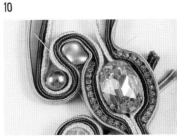

11. Make four leaves with fuchsia pearls (see instructions on pages 28–29). Use cords that are 8cm (3¼in) long.

11

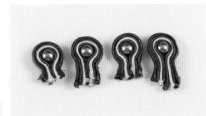

12

13

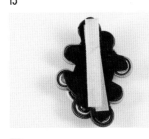

12. Sew the leaves on to the back of the main motif to create the design shown, left. Sew 1cm (½in) of green rhinestone chain between the two coils.

13. Glue Alcantara on to the back of the piece and cut off the excess. Attach the self-adhesive hook and loop and fix the piece to the headband.

The finished headband.

DAYTIME HEADBAND

Materials

* 70CM (27½IN) SOUTACHE CORD IN DARK GREEN, FUCHSIA, YELLOW, DARK PINK, LIGHT GREEN, LILAC, METALLIC PINK, PURPLE AND BRONZE
* 1.4M (4½FT) SOUTACHE CORD IN MID-GREEN
* HEADBAND
* 11 METALLIC ROSES IN VARIOUS COLOURS
* JEWELLERY GLUE
* THREADS IN MATCHING COLOURS
* SCISSORS
* HOT GLUE

1. Take a length of dark green cord and varnish the ends. Thread the needle and tie a knot. Take one end of the cord, fold it over and, making sure the end is at what will be the back of the piece, stitch it to secure.

2. Wind the cord around itself with a few stitches between the cords to secure each wrap. Take care not to let the thread show on the front of the work.

3. When finished, take the cord to the back and secure it with hidden stitches. Cut the 1.4m (4½ft) of cord into two and make two coils. Coil the other colours. Place a contrasting colour rose to the centre of each coil and glue them in place. Finally, glue the coil shapes on to the headband using hot glue.

1

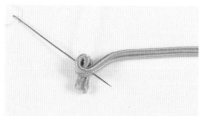

2

3

The finished headband.

ELEGANT EVENING HEADBAND

Materials

* 2M (6½FT) SOUTACHE CORD IN PURPLE AND APPLE GREEN
* HEADBAND
* 2 20MM (¾IN) DIAMETER YELLOW AND ORANGE SWAROVSKI CABOCHON
* 2 8MM (¼IN) DIAMETER ORANGE SWAROVSKI CRYSTALS
* 2 12MM (½IN) DIAMETER GREEN SWAROVSKI RIVOLI CRYSTALS IN BEZELS
* 10CM (4IN) RHINESTONE CHAIN
* 15 X 15CM (6 X 6IN) PURPLE ALCANTARA
* MATCHING NYMO THREAD
* SCISSORS
* BEADING NEEDLE
* JEWELLERY GLUE

1. Divide the cords into 50cm (19¾in) lengths. Cut a 5cm (2in) strip from the Alcantara. Spread glue on the back of the cabochon and fix it to the Alcantara. Wait for it to dry, Thread the needle and tie a knot. Seal the ends of the cords with varnish. Leave an end of 3cm (1¼in) free and stitch the cords together in the middle. Place a cabochon next to the cords and sew the cords once all the way around the cabochon (see pages 24–25). Complete a circle, return to the beginning of the stitching and overlap the cords slightly. Cut off the excess Alcantara around the cabochon.

2. Bend the cords round to the back of the work without cutting them and stitch them in place. Coil the cords and bring them back to the front of the piece. Stitch them in place and form a new coil.

3. Return the cords to the back of the piece. Cut 4cm (1½in) from the rhinestone chain and sew the chain to the coil with small hidden stitches.

4. Bring the loose cords to the front of the piece and sew them around the chain.

1

2

3

4

5. When you reach the end of the chain, stitch in an orange crystal. Curve and stitch the cords to secure. Insert a green Rivoli crystal in the curve and sew the cords to the crystal through the holes. Secure all the cords at the base of the crystal with a few stitches. Curve the cords to the left, insert an orange crystal, then pass the needle through the hole in the crystal from the outside inwards, twice. Secure cords at the back of the piece.

6. Spread glue on the back of the piece and fix it to the Alcantara, making sure it adheres well.

When dry, cut off the excess Alcantara. Make the other piece symmetrically. Glue both pieces to the headband.

The finished headband.

5

6

CREATIONS IN RUBBER

BRACELET AND EARRINGS

Materials

* 2M (6½FT) PURPLE SOUTACHE CORD
* 1M (3FT) MUSTARD AND ORANGE SOUTACHE CORD
* 2.5M (8FT) FUCHSIA TUBULAR RUBBER
* 2 8MM (½IN) DIAMETER ORANGE CABOCHONS IN BEZELS
* 30CM (11¾IN) ORANGE RHINESTONE CHAIN
* 4 ORANGE CUBIC CRYSTALS
* 6 3MM DIAMETER PURPLE CRYSTALS
* 15CM (6IN) CIRCUMFERENCE PLASTIC TUBE
* 15MM (½IN) CIRCUMFERENCE PLASTIC TUBE
* 2 EAR WIRES
* 2 HOOKS FOR EARWIRES
* JEWELLERY GLUE
* SCISSORS
* ADHESIVE TAPE
* BEADING NEEDLE
* 2 JUMP RINGS
* 1 SPRING CLASP
* 2 GRIP BANDS

Bracelet

1. Cut three lengths of 18cm (7in) from the fuchsia tubular rubber and secure them at one end with a piece of adhesive tape to keep them together (this will be removed at the end). Glue the three cords to the middle piece of tubing and wind the cords once around it. Fix the three cords again with glue where they overlap. Keep the cords flat.

2. Turn over the piece. Wind the cords around the left-hand rubber tubing, then move the cords under the central tubing, towards the right hand tubing, to form a figure-eight of sorts.

1

2

3

3. Wind the cords around the right-hand tubing, then pass the cord over and around the middle tubing and back towards the left-hand tubing again. Place the cords slightly lower on the tubing every time you wrap.

4. Carry on weaving in the same way until you reach the end of the tubing (inset). Fix the work at the back with a drop of glue.

5. Attach the grip bands, the two jump rings and the spring clasp to the ends (see also inset).

4

5

Earring

1

Making the basic hoop

1. Cut two lengths of rubber, one 11cm (4¼in) and one 14cm (5½in). Glue the two ends on each length of tubing to make a hoop.

2. Cut 70cm (27½in) of purple cord, glue it to the bigger hoop and wrap it around a couple of times. Place the small hoop inside the big hoop. Pass the cord under the large hoop, over the small hoop, then under the small hoop again, wrap the cord around the small hoop and bring it out between the two hoops. Alternate this wrapping action, moving in between the hoops each time to pass from the small to the large and vice versa. Wrap until the cord is used up and secure the ends.

2a

2b

2c

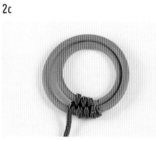

2d

Making the embellishment hoop

1. Fix one end of the mustard cord to the 15mm (½in) circumference plastic tube with a drop of glue. Wrap the cord around the tube to make a complete circle.

2. Cut off the excess and stick the ends together (inset).

3. Repeat steps 2 and 3 with the orange cord.

1

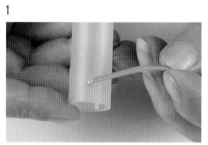

2

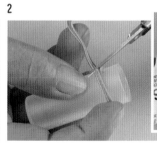

3

4. Attach the rhinestone chain to the orange cord, taking care to keep the links close together. Make sure the beads stay upright and do not lie flat. Do not use too much glue, as this will make the work slippery. If this happens, wipe off the excess glue immediately.

5. Spread a layer of glue on the outside edge of the chain and attach the purple cord.

6. Leave the piece to dry well, then carefully slide it off the plastic tube. Place it on a flat surface and straighten it out if necessary.

7. Cut the embellishment hoop at the point where it is glued, insert it inside the rubber hoop, then glue the opening back up again to close the circle. Position the embellishment hoop within the basic hoop as shown, next to the purple cord, and fix it in place with a drop of glue.

4

5

6

7

Flat piece

1. Cut 20cm (7¾in) lengths of cord in mustard, orange and purple. Place the cabochon in the middle of the mustard cord, spread a layer of glue around the edge of the cabochon and stick the cord to it. Using the gluing technique for cords (see pages 46–47), glue the two remaining cords in place.

2. Follow the basic technique instructions on pages 20–23 to secure the two purple beads in place.

3. Secure the cords on the back of the piece.

1

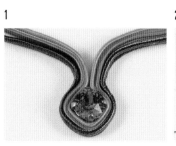

2

3

4. Glue the flat piece to the top of the embellishment hoop as shown, right. Attach the ear wires by inserting the ear wire ring between the cords. Flatten the cord and cut off any excess. Hook the earwire on to the ring. Cut a matching piece of Alcantara, glue it to the back of the earring and when dry cut off any excess.

Repeat the whole process to make a second earring.

The same rubber earring in a different colour combination.

EARRINGS

LARGE HOOP EARRINGS WITH A DROP

1. Cut four lengths of 30cm (11¾in) from the cords: two aquamarine, one green and one turquoise. Thread the needle and make a knot. Take the two aquamarine cords, leave 10cm (4in) hanging on one side and sew the two cords to the cabochon through the holes in the bezel (inset). Go back through the holes again to secure. Attach the remaining cords in the same way.

2. Stitch the cords together at the base of the cabochon. Divide the eight cords into two groups. Curve the 10cm (4in) lengths away from the base, insert a 10mm (½in) turquoise crystal to the left of the cabochon and sew in place. Secure the cords to the back of the piece, cut off the excess and varnish the ends.

3. Curve the right-hand cords and secure with a few stitches. Insert another 10mm (½in) turquoise crystal passing the needle to the other side of the cords through the hole in the crystal, return through the hole from the outside inwards and secure it. Create another curve and insert a rhinestone ball. Wrap the cords around the ball, stitch it, and then secure the cords at the back (inset).

4. For the pendant, make a few stitches between the two right-hand coils. Thread two 4mm diameter crystals, a Venetian glass drop, and a 4mm diameter crystal on to the needle and pass it to the outside, then back through the drop and the two crystals. Secure the drop element to the bottom of the two right coils.

5. Cut 5cm (2in) lengths from the cords: two in aquamarine, one in turquoise and one in green. Place the cords together in the following order, left to right: turquoise, aquamarine and green. Sew the cords together in the middle. Curve the cords in half to make the shape of a teardrop. Sew the teardrop on to the bottom of the motif between the two central coils (inset).

Materials

* 1.6M (5½FT) SOUTACHE CORD IN AQUAMARINE, GREEN AND TURQUOISE
* 2 18 X 13MM (¾ X ½IN) DIAMETER SWAROVSKI CRYSTALS
* 2 TURQUOISE CABOCHONS WITH BEZEL
* 4 10MM (½IN) DIAMETER TURQUOISE CRYSTALS
* 2 10MM (½IN) DIAMETER RHINESTONE CRYSTAL BALLS
* 2 VENETIAN GLASS DROPS WITH TURQUOISE FLORAL DECORATION
* 6 4MM DIAMETER CRYSTALS
* 2 EAR WIRES
* 50CM (19¾IN) LENGTH OF RHINESTONE CHAIN
* JEWELLERY GLUE
* NYMO THREAD IN MATCHING COLOUR
* BEADING NEEDLE
* CLEAR NAIL VARNISH
* SCISSORS
* CLIPPERS
* 20 X 20CM (7¾ X 7¾IN) ALCANTARA IN MATCHING COLOUR
* 15CM (6IN) CIRCUMFERENCE PLASTIC TUBE

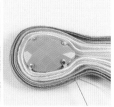

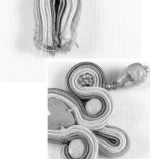

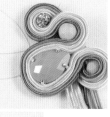

6. For the outer hoop, use the gluing technique (see pages 46–47). Glue the end of the aquamarine cord to the plastic tube and wrap the cord around the tube once to form a complete circle. Fix the end to the initial gluing point. Cut off any excess cord.

7. Repeat again with the same colour. Continue in the following way: place a drop of glue at the point where you started the first circle; use a toothpick to control the amount of glue you apply, so that it does not leak to the front of the work; stick the new cord on to the existing one. Glue around the entire circumference of the hoop and cut off any excess cord at the end.

6

7

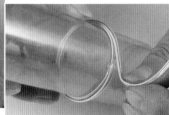

8. Repeat step 6 with the rhinestone chain, taking care that the links are kept close together. Keep the chain upright so that the crystals are straight. Do not use too much glue, as this can make the work slippery. If this happens, immediately remove the excess glue. Spread a layer of glue on the upper part of the chain, and glue the turquoise cord to the chain. Glue the green cord on to the turquoise cord in the same way as in step 7.

9. When the hoop is dry, slowly slide it off the plastic tube, with the help of the tip of a pair of scissors. Place the loop on a flat surface and flatten it out if necessary.

10. Position the motif at the joining point of the aquamarine hoop and glue it in place.

11. Spread a layer of glue on the back of the frame of the earring and fix it to the Alcantara. Make sure the work adheres and leave it to dry. Cut off the excess Alcantara fabric and attach the ear wire.

Repeat the whole process to make a second earring.

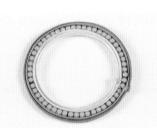
8

9

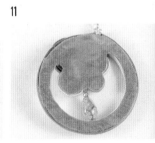
10

11

One finished earring.

EARRINGS WITH A STONE CABOCHON

Materials

* 1.3M (4½FT) OF SOUTACHE CORD IN AQUAMARINE, TURQUOISE AND PURPLE
* 2 PURPLE STONE CABOCHONS IN BEZELS
* 2 14MM (½IN) DIAMETER PURPLE SWAROVSKI RIVOLI CABOCHONS IN BEZELS
* 30CM (11¾IN) TURQUOISE RHINESTONE CHAIN
* 4 10MM (½IN) DIAMETER TURQUOISE CRYSTALS
* 2 8MM (¼IN) DIAMETER TURQUOISE RHINESTONE BALLS
* 2 4MM DIAMETER PURPLE PEARLS
* 2 EAR WIRES
* TURQUOISE AND PURPLE NYMO THREAD
* BEADING NEEDLE
* SCISSORS
* GLUE
* CLEAR NAIL VARNISH
* 10 X 10CM (4 X 4IN) ALCANTARA IN MATCHING COLOUR

1. Cut 30cm (11¾in) lengths from the cords: two purple and one in the other two colours. Spread a layer of glue on the back of one stone cabochon, fix it to the Alcantara and wait for it to dry. Take the two purple cords and curve them around the cabochon, leaving 10cm (4in) of cord hanging at either side. Sew the cords to the back of the cabochon and the Alcantara using purple thread. Sew the cabochon in place and return to the start of the work. Do not cut the thread.

2. Cut a 15cm (6in) length of rhinestone chain. Attach it to the purple cords, sewing between the rhinestones. Keep the stones in the chain close together so that they do not fan out. At the end, secure the chain with a few stitches.

1
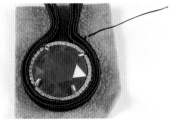

2

3. Curve the blue cords around the purple cords, leaving 10cm (4in) hanging on either side. Sew the cords together around the cabochon.

4. Sew a purple pearl to the base of the cabochon as shown. Curve the cords on the right and fix in place with purple thread stitches. Sew in a turquoise crystal, pass the needle through the hole in the crystal to secure it and sew along the cords for about 1cm (½in). Coil the remaining loose cords without inserting any pearls. Take the cord ends to the back of the work (inset) but do not cut them.

3
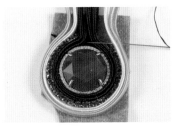

4

5. Change to the turquoise thread, With the two purple, one turquoise and one aquamarine cords, make a spiral around the coil you have just made. Secure the completed spiral with small stitches on the back of the piece. Sew the cords to the back.

6. Repeat the instructions in step 4 to insert and secure a crystal on the left of the piece. Curve the cords again and insert a rhinestone ball in the second coil. Take the cords to the back and secure them with a few stitches.

7. Cut two 20cm (7¾in) lengths from the turquoise and aquamarine cords, then cut them in half so you have four lengths of 10cm (4in) lengths in each colour. Double up the turquoise and aquamarine cords and sew them to the coil around the rhinestone ball. After sewing, secure the cords to the back of the work.

5

6

7

8. Take the leftover cords in all three colours and sew them around a purple Rivoli cabochon through the holes in the bezel. Sew the cords together at the base of the cabochon.

9. Glue the motif you have made in step 8 to the bottom of the motif created in step 7, between the two coils. Attach the ear wire, glue the whole motif on to the Alcantara and cut off the excess fabric to finish.

8

9

NOTE
Create the second earring following the same steps, taking care to invert the position of the coils so that a mirrored motif is made for the second earring.

One finished earring.

EARRINGS WITH LEAVES

1. Cut a 10cm (4in) length from the metallic blue cord and seal with varnish at both ends, Sew the cord twice around a crystal. Take the cord to the back and secure with some small stitches (inset).

2. Cut a 15cm (6in) length of the small rhinestone chain and sew it to the metallic blue cord, making sure there are no gaps.

Materials

* 2M (6½FT) SOUTACHE CORD IN AQUAMARINE, TURQUOISE, LIGHT PURPLE AND METALLIC BLUE
* 6 10MM (½IN) DIAMETER CRYSTALS
* 2 12MM (½IN) DIAMETER TURQUOISE SWAROVSKI CABOCHONS IN BEZEL
* 35CM (13¾IN) SMALL RHINESTONE CHAIN
* 50CM (19¾IN) TURQUOISE BEAD CHAIN
* 4 TURQUOISE GLASS DROPS
* NYMO THREAD IN MATCHING COLOUR
* 10CM (4IN) CIRCUMFERENCE PLASTIC TUBE
* BEADING NEEDLE
* JEWELLERY GLUE
* 20 X 20CM (7¾ X 7¾IN) OF TURQUOISE ALCANTARA
* 2 EAR WIRES
* SCISSORS
* FLAT-NOSE PLIERS
* PINS

3. Take the aquamarine cord and coil it twice around the chain. Secure at the back of the motif and cut off the excess cord. In the same way, add a layer of turquoise cord and a layer of purple cord (inset). Secure well.

4. For the leaves, cut four lengths of 10cm (4in) from the aquamarine and turquoise cord. Sew two of the double lengths around two glass drops to form leaves, following the leaf technique on pages 28–29.

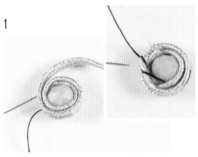

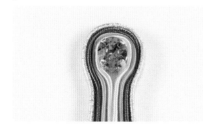

5. Cut 16cm (6¼in) lengths from each colour of cord, curve in half and sew the cords to a turquoise cabochon through the bezel holes. Sew the cords at the base of the cabochon with small stitches. You will now have a group of eight cords all 6cm (2½in) long at the base of the cabochon.

5. Divide the cords into two groups. On both sides of the cabochon, curve the cords, insert a turquoise crystal, coil the cords around the crystal and sew in position (see pages 20–23). Secure the cords to the back of the piece (inset).

6. Cut two 10cm (4in) lengths of aquamarine cord. Fix it to the plastic tube with a little glue and wrap the cord round the tube. Build up the hoop as shown in steps 6 to 9 on page 83, layering the turquoise cord, a length of turquoise bead chain, and purple and metallic blue cords (inset).

5

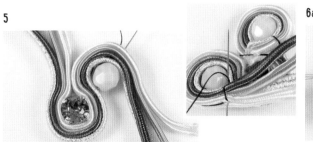

6a

7. Once the hoop is made, pin the two leaves and other pieces in place as shown, or as you prefer. Fix the pieces to the hoop with glue. Glue Alcantara on to the reverse of the piece, trim to size and thread in the ear wire to finish (7d).

7a

7b

7c

7d

NOTE
Make the second earring following the same steps, but in a mirror image to the first earring.

One finished earring.

HAIR COMBS

WHITE HAIR COMB

Materials

* 1.5M (5FT) SOUTACHE CORD IN MOTHER OF PEARL WHITE
* 1M (3½FT) SOUTACHE CORD IN METALLIC WHITE
* 2 10MM (½IN) DIAMETER PEARLS
* 2 6MM (¼IN) DIAMETER PEARLS
* 1 4MM DIAMETER PEARL
* 30CM (11¾IN) WHITE RHINESTONE CHAIN
* 1 15 X 18MM (½ X ¾IN) WHITE SWAROVSKI TEARDROP CRYSTAL IN BEZEL
* 1 HAIR COMB
* NYMO THREAD IN WHITE
* BEADING NEEDLE
* CLEAR NAIL VARNISH
* 10CM (4IN) CIRCUMFERENCE PLASTIC TUBE
* SCISSORS
* DOUBLE-SIDED ADHESIVE TAPE

1. Cut three lengths of 20cm (7¼in) cord: two in mother of pearl white and one in metallic white. Seal the ends with varnish. Position the cords lengthways with the metallic white in the middle. Curve the cords so they are at equal lengths on both sides. Place the bezel 7cm (2¾in) from the top curve of the cords and sew it to the cords through the holes (inset).

2. Insert a 4mm pearl at the base of the bezel, and sew the cords together through the pearl. Sew back through the cords and the small pearl again to make sure it is secure.

3. Pass the needle to the outside of one set of cords, curve the cords around a 6mm (¼in) pearl, and sew the pearl to the cords. Pass the needle through the cords and the pearl to the other side, and repeat with another 6mm (¼in) pearl. Take the cords to the back of the piece and secure them with small stitches. Cut off the excess cords.

4. Insert the white teardrop crystal in the bezel and secure it by closing the four prongs. The inset photograph shows how the piece should look on the reverse.

1

2

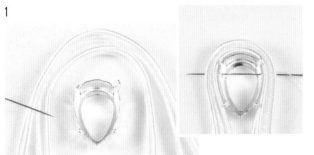

3

4

5. To make the curved, coiled piece, cut four 30cm (11¾in) lengths: three from the mother of pearl white cord, one from the metallic white cord. Cut one 15cm (6in) length from the rhinestone chain. Apply a drop of glue to the plastic tube. Leaving 8cm (3¼in) of mother of pearl white cord hanging, attach it to the glue and wrap it once round the tube, without adding more glue. Do not cut the excess cord. Repeat the process with the metallic white cord and with the mother of pearl white cord again, leaving 8cm (3¼in) hanging at the start each time. Glue the white rhinestone chain on top of the other layers and cut off the excess. Finally, glue a last length of mother of pearl white cord to the chain, without cutting off the excess. Carefully slide the hoop off the tube. Cut the hoop in half so that you have two semicircles with 8cm (3¼in) hanging at the ends from each of the four cords. Take one of the two semicircles, curve the hanging cords upwards, insert a pearl and form a coil. Fix the cords at the rear with some stitches. Repeat with the other semicircle.

5

6

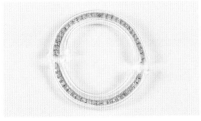

7

8

9

6. Use the plastic tube to make another hoop in the same sequence as per step 4, but without leaving any excess cord at the beginning or at the end. Slide the finished hoop off the tube and cut it in half.

7. Cut a piece of double-sided adhesive tape and stick it on to the back of the comb so that it is hidden. Place one semicircle on the central part of the comb, securing it with two stitches to the double-sided adhesive tape.

8. Position the two coils so that they meet in the centre, and adjust them to the size and shape of the comb, cutting any excess coil if necessary.

9. Position the crystal in the centre and fix in place with a drop of glue. Apply glue to the back of the work too, at the overlapping points of the components to secure them.

The finished comb.

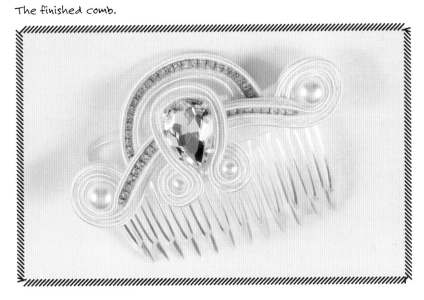

TURQUOISE AND AQUAMARINE HAIR COMB

1. Cut 25cm (9¾in) lengths of aquamarine, metallic blue and turquoise cords. Curve the cords round the blue oval cabochon, making sure the cords are even on both sides. Begin to sew the aquamarine and metallic blue cords to the cabochon 8cm (3¼in) from the top, going through the holes in the bezel. Do not cut the threads when you finish sewing.

2. Cut 15cm (6in) from the rhinestone chain and, starting at the base of the cabochon, sew it to the cords, stitching between the rhinestones. Make sure to keep the rhinestones close together and upright.

3. Sew the turquoise cord on to the rhinestone chain. Place the bicone crystal at the base of the cabochon and sew together the cords and the bicone crystal. Sew through the bicone crystal and cords twice to make sure they are secure.

4. Curve all the cords to the left, and make small stitches to secure the curve. Insert the white 10mm (½in) diameter crystal in the curve. Sew through the hole in the crystal and come out on the side of the cabochon. Pull the thread to close the coil and secure the crystal in place with small hidden stitches. Pass the needle back through the crystal and through the six outer cords. Repeat. At the end, secure the cords to the back of the piece.

Materials

* 1.5M (5FT) SOUTACHE CORD IN TURQUOISE
* 75CM (29½IN) SOUTACHE CORD IN METALLIC BLUE
* 50CM (19¾IN) SOUTACHE CORD IN AQUAMARINE
* 30CM (11¾IN) TURQUOISE RHINESTONE CHAIN
* 1 15 X 18MM (½ X ¾IN) BLUE OVAL CABOCHON IN BEZEL
* 1 14MM (½IN) DIAMETER RIVOLI CABOCHON IN BEZEL
* 1 12MM (½IN) DIAMETER VITRAL BLUE RIVOLI CABOCHON IN BEZEL
* 3 8MM (¼IN) DIAMETER WHITE CRYSTALS
* 3 8MM (¼IN) DIAMETER PEARLS
* 1 10MM (½IN) DIAMETER WHITE CRYSTAL
* 1 6MM (¼IN) DIAMETER WHITE BICONE CRYSTAL
* 2 6MM (¼IN) DIAMETER BLUE BRIOLETTE CRYSTALS
* 1 12MM (½IN) DIAMETER BLUE CRYSTAL PENDANT
* 1 OPEN RING
* NYMO THREAD IN MATCHING COLOUR
* SCISSORS
* GLUE
* 1 HAIR COMB
* 1 BEADING NEEDLE
* 10 X 10CM (4 X 4IN) ALCANTARA IN MATCHING COLOUR

1

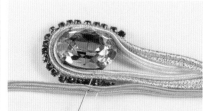

3

2

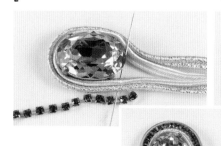

4

5. Cut four 25cm (9¾in) lengths of cord: three turquoise and one metallic blue. Set the 14mm (½in)diameter Rivoli cabochon using the same technique used for the oval cabochon. Place the cords in the following order: two turquoise cords, the remaining rhinestone chain, one metallic blue cord and, lastly, the other turquoise cord. When you have finished sewing the cords, insert a blue briolette crystal between the two groups of two cords. Coil the cords to the right and secure them at the back of the work with stitches.

5

6a

6b

6c

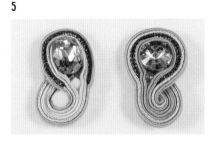

6d

6. Cut three 25cm (9¾in) lengths of each cord. Sew the cords around the Rivoli crystal, through the holes in the bezel, starting 10cm (4in) from the beginning of the cord. After sewing, gather the cords at the base. Sew the three cords together on one side, insert a blue briolette crystal and sew the next three cords. Sew through again to secure the crystal in place. Using the zigzag technique (see pages 32–33), create the motifs with three crystals on one side and three pearls on the other. When this is done, take the cords to the back of the piece and secure everything with small stitches (6d).

7. Take the two cabochon pieces and spread a little glue on the back of one of them. Fix them together as shown. Overlap them slightly so that they adhere well.

8. Sew the zigzag piece to the cabochon piece. After sewing, brush a layer of glue on the back of the piece. Place it on the Alcantara and press lightly so that it adheres well. Cut off any excess thread. Attach the blue crystal pendant to the Alcantara with the ring. Spread a layer of glue on the hair comb and glue the whole piece on to the comb. Leave to dry.

7

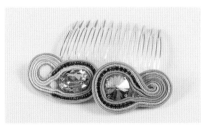

8

The finished comb.

LAMPSHADE

1. Cut an 8 x 8cm (3¼ x 3¼in) square of Alcantara. Cut eight 30cm (11¾in) lengths of cord, two in each colour. Spread a layer of glue on the back of the cabochon, and press it firmly to the Alcantara.

2. Make two small marks on the Alcantara at the centre top and bottom of the cabochon to mark its position. Place the dark green cord at one mark leaving 10cm (4in) hanging. Begin to sew the cord around the cabochon close to its edge, entering and exiting the cord and the Alcantara. Sew the cord around to the second mark. Repeat the process on the other side.

3. Layer the other three light green, cream and magenta cords alongside the cord you have just sewn. Pass the needle through the Alcantara and cords to the front of the piece and secure the three cords next to the first one. Pass the needle to the back of the piece through the Alcantara. Repeat these two steps for half the circumference. Take the thread to the back of the Alcantara, move to the other side of the cabochon and continue in the same way to attach the other three cords on the other side of the cabochon (inset).

1

2

3

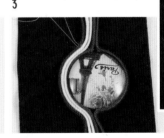

4. After sewing, cut off the excess thread and Alcantara. Sew the cords together at both ends of the cabochon with a few stitches (inset).

5. Divide the cords into two groups, curve one set away from the base of the cabochon and stitch. Sew a crystal to the cords, ensuring that no kinks form in the cords during sewing. Go

back through the crystal and the cords to secure.

4

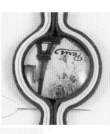

5

6. Take the thread to the right of the cabochon and repeat step 5 on the other side. Make another curve and insert a crystal ball.

Turn the piece around 180 degrees and repeat steps 5 and 6 with the sets of cords at the other end of the cabochon.

6a

6b

6c

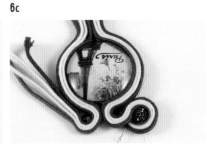

7. Cut a 30cm (11¾in) length of cord in each colour. Layer the cords in the following order, left to right: dark green, light green, cream and magenta. Fold the cords in half so the magenta cord is in the middle.

Sew the centres of the cords together for 2mm (½in). Sew the eight cords together for 2cm (¾in) (inset). You now have the tip of a leaf.

8. Separate the cords into two groups and place a crystal in the centre. Sew it in place with the cords (inset). Sew the eight cords together for 5mm (½in).

7

8

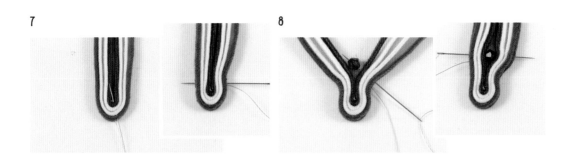

9. Repeat step 8 to place the second crystal. Continue this process until six crystals have been placed. Finish the piece with two coils containing two

more crystals, as shown. Secure the cords at the back of the piece. Follow steps 7 and 8 to make a second, identical piece.

9a

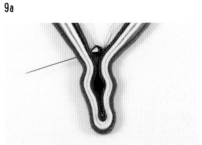

9b

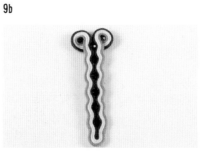

9c

10. Cut four 25cm (9¾in) lengths from each colour cord. Make four further pieces following steps 7, 8 and 9, placing five crystals within the length and one in each final coil.

11. Cut six pieces of Alcantara and glue them to the back of the pieces over the stitching. Cut six 1cm (½in) pieces of hook and loop fastening and glue them to the back of the long pieces you have made. Position the cabochon on the lampshade and arrange the other pieces around it in a neat pattern.

10   **11**

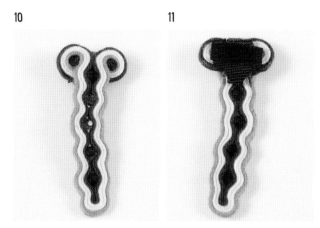

Detail of the finished piece.

BROOCHES
FOR HATS

HAT BROOCH

Materials

* 1.5M (5FT) SOUTACHE CORD IN METALLIC PINK, DARK PINK, PURPLE
* 2 20MM (¾IN) DIAMETER PINK CABOCHONS IN BEZELS
* 10 6MM (¼IN) DIAMETER PURPLE PEARLS
* 2 6MM (¼IN) DIAMETER PINK RHINESTONE BALLS
* 16 6MM (¼IN) DIAMETER PINK SWAROVSKI CRYSTALS
* 2 6MM (¼IN) LILAC BICONE CRYSTALS
* MATCHING NYMO THREAD
* BEADING NEEDLE
* 20 X 20CM (7¾ X 7¾IN) ALCANTARA IN MATCHING COLOUR
* TRACING PAPER
* FELT TIP PEN
* BROOCH BACK
* 30CM (11¾IN) RHINESTONE CHAIN
* JEWELLERY GLUE

1. Cut a square of Alcantara 5 x 5cm (2 x 2in). Cut three 25cm (9¾in) and three 30cm (11¾in) lengths of metallic pink, dark pink, purple and a 15cm (6in) length of rhinestone chain.

2. Take the pink cabochon, spread a layer of glue on the back, place it centrally on the Alcantara and ensure it adheres well.

3. Make a mark on the Alcantara halfway around the circumference of the cabochon. Take the three 25cm (9¾in) cords and position vertically in the following order, left to right: purple, dark pink, metallic pink. Fold the cords in half and make a few stitches in the centre of the fold. Curve the cords

around the top of the cabochon, with the stitching on the mark made previously. Sew the cords to the cabochon through the bezel (inset).

4. At the base of the cabochon, place a bicone crystal and sew all the cords and the crystal together. Make two coils with purple pearls on either

side of the bicone crystal, with a third purple pearl between the two coils, under the crystal. Cut off the excess Alcantara. Secure the cords to the back and cut off the excess (inset). You have created a basic element (see pages 20–23).

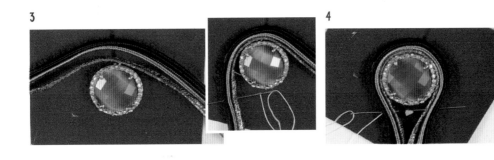

5. Cut the rhinestone chain in two. Take one length and place it around the purple cord on the outside of the piece. Sew it in place, stitching between the rhinestones, and secure the ends well.

6. Sew three 30cm (11¾in) cord lengths on to the rhinestone chain. Finish sewing at the point where the chain meets the coils. Form two new coils around the purple pearls, one on either side of the existing coils.

Make sure the new coils are level with the previous ones (inset). Repeat the process from step 1 to make a second, identical piece.

5

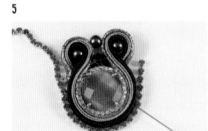

6

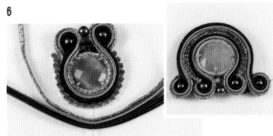

7. Cut 15cm (6in) lengths of metallic pink, dark pink and purple cord. Create a 5cm (2in) curve with the purple cord in the middle, and sew in the centre with a few hidden stitches. Insert a pink crystal and sew in place between the cords. Go back through the hole in the crystal to secure it more firmly. Sew the six layers of cord with a couple of stitches at the base of the crystal to make sure they are firmly fixed. On the right side fold the cords downwards. Stitch back through all nine layers of cord (inset).

7

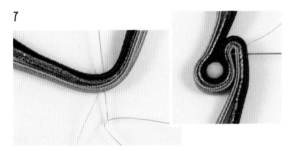

8. Make a new curve with the right-hand cords so that the top of the curves are level. Place another pink crystal in the curve and sew the crystal in place between the cords (see wave technique on pages 30–31).

9. Repeat step 8 to place a third pink crystal. At the end, secure the cords with stitches. Cut off any excess and seal the ends with varnish. You now have a piece comprising three waves and three crystals.

10. Make another three identical pieces following steps 7 to 9.

8

9

10

11. Make four leaves with pink crystals and two leaves with rhinestone balls, using the leaf technique on pages 28–29.

12. Cut two 50cm (19¾in) lengths of metallic pink cord and make two 2cm (¾in)-diameter coils (see also inset).

13. Cut two 5cm (2in) lengths of cord in each colour. Gather them into two groups and curve them as shown, with the purple in the middle, and sew together with hidden stitches along the entire length.

11

12

13

14. To assemble, take one of the two cabochon pieces. Spread a layer of glue at the base of three of the leaves from step 10, and fix them on the back of the cabochon piece, starting next to a coil. Press down lightly to fix securely. Repeat on the other side (see inset).

15. Sew two small leaves on either side of a rhinestone ball leaf from step 10. Repeat for the other rhinestone ball leaf.

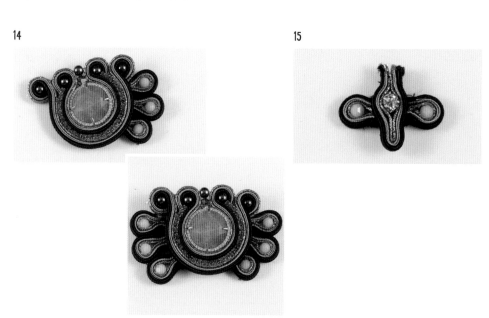

14

15

16. Sew one rhinestone ball leaf from step 14 to the top-centre of one of the cabochon pieces. Sew a curved cord (see step 13) to the back of the piece behind the rhinestone leaf (inset). Repeat on the other cabochon piece.

17. Sew the two coils. Spread a layer of glue on one half of the coils and fix one cabochon piece on to them as shown. Leave to dry well and repeat on the other side, with the other piece, leaving a small space between them in the middle where the coils can be seen.

Note: We have used a different colour motif from step 17 onwards to demonstrate the variety of soutache embellishments you can make using these directions.

16

17

18

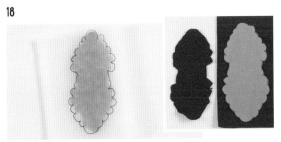

18. Place a sheet of tracing paper on the back of the finished work and with a felt tip pen trace the outline of the piece. Use sharp scissors to cut out the shape you have traced. Place it on the Alcantara and cut round it carefully. You now have a new shape in Alcantara (inset).

19. Make two small cuts on the Alcantara, where you want to attach the brooch back. Pin the brooch back to the Alcantara.

20. Glue the Alcantara shape and fix it to the back of the piece, making sure no glue seeps to the front.

19

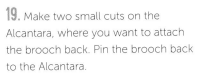 

20

The finished piece.

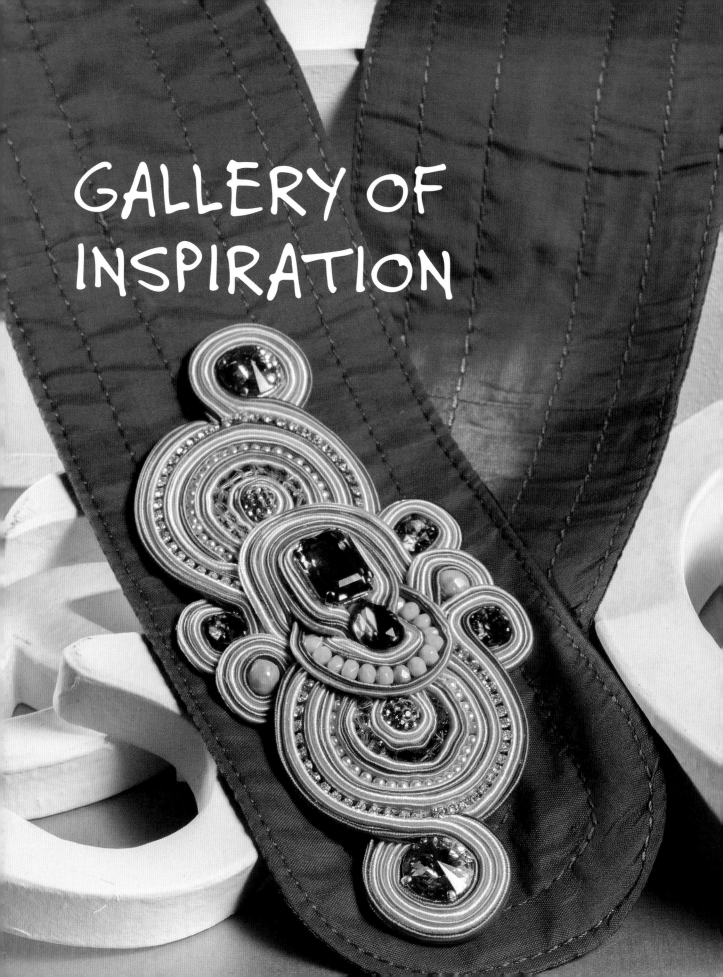

GALLERY OF
INSPIRATION

Vintage-style decorations with elegant details can be used to embellish velvet bags and small clutch bags, suitable for all occasions. The brooch fastener on the back of the piece allows it to be used as an accessory on hats and coats, too, for a personal style, that adds a touch of glamour.

The fastener on the belt, left, is made from cords in various shades of turquoise and purple, together with wonderful complementary Swarovski crystals. It is also an ideal accessory on a dress for a special occasion.

Elegant, dazzling ballet pumps
embellished with soutache weaves,
rhinestone chains and matching
crystals are just irresistible and
perfect for a special evening.

These flip-flops, wonderfully decorated with soutache embellishments, remind us of summer and Capri fashion. They are perfect to wear as a stylish item for an evening by the sea or for a romantic dinner.

Create eye-catching earrings with soutache. Using the techniques I have explained in this book, you will be able to make many styles in all your favourite colours. They are just right for both daytime and evening wear.

Nostalgia for vintage items inspired these necklaces made with soutache cord and Swarovski crystals, pearls and briolette crystals in many hues. They can be worn with any outfit.

The exotic soutache fastener, worked in turquoise, purple and aquamarine cords, complements this stylish crocheted chenille bag perfectly!

These trendy crochet slippers are given an extra spark of panache with stunning soutache embellishments reminiscent of a peacock's plumage, complete with rhinestone chains and iridescent cabochons.